The Sources of American
Student Activism

The Sources of American Student Activism

James L. Wood
University of California
Riverside

Lexington Books
D.C. Heath and Company
Lexington, Massachusetts
Toronto   London

Library of Congress Cataloging in Publication Data

Wood, James L.   1941-
   The sources of American student activism.

   Bibliography: p.
   1. Student movements—United States—History. I. Title
LA229.W66   371.8'1   73-23020
ISBN 0-669-92478-4

Copyright © 1974 by D.C. Heath and Company

Published simultaneously in Canada.

Printed in the United States of America.

International Standard Book Number: 0-669-92478-4

Library of Congress Catalog Card Number: 73-23020

To Patsy

whose emotional and intellectual
support is evident throughout
this book

Contents

List of Tables

Acknowledgments

There are many intellectual and other related debts that one accumulates in the process of writing a book. This is especially the case when the project begins as a Ph.D. dissertation. I have accumulated many such debts, and I would like to record them now.

Among those who influenced the development and direction of this book, Neil J. Smelser stands out. He read and extensively commented on every chapter in the book. As others who are acquainted with him will appreciate, these comments were of the highest intellectual order. The book is considerably improved because of his efforts. Over the years I have had various associations with Professor Smelser, and I have thoroughly enjoyed and profited from my relationship with him.

I was also fortunate to receive many comments from Robert Blauner and Robert H. Somers. I especially benefited from Blauner's comments on the concept of political consciousness and on the topic of political ideology in general. Somers was especially helpful with regard to issues involving the student movement, as well as with statistical problems. I owe a very special debt to Dr. Somers. He permitted me to use the data on U.C. Berkeley students that he collected in 1968 as well as his parental data that had never been previously analyzed. His 1968 study was a follow-up of his 1964 study of the Free Speech Movement, which was probably the first systematic study of the New Left. Without these data, this book would be considerably different. I am similarly indebted to Dr. Jeanne Block of the Institute of Human Development at U.C. Berkeley for permitting me to use her parental data for secondary analysis.

The author of a book on student politics accrues a special advantage by being at Berkeley: there are always a number of people who have ideas about student activism. I have been privileged to receive comments from the following people: Charles Y. Glock, Gertrude Jaeger, Gary T. Marx, Herbert Blumer, John A. Clausen, Milton Mankoff, Allen H. Barton, Arthur L. Stinchcombe, Seymour Martin Lipset, C. Norman Alexander, Morris Rosenberg, Alphonso Pinkney, David Swift, Peter Ekeh, Maurice Manel, Manly Horowitz, Sue Gallup, Ayad Al-Qazzaz, Paul Wong, Jean-Guy Vaillancourt, Bob Michels, Irwin Sperber, Diane D'Agostino, Ruth Dixon, Dain Oliver, Hardy Frye, Pam Lee, Norma Wikler, Steve Long-staff, Barbara Ballis Lal, and Gail Omvedt. In addition, I had the opportunity to talk over the comments with many of these people, which was always very helpful.

Paul Wong deserves a special comment with regard to this project. When we were both graduate students at Berkeley, Paul invited me to give a paper with him at the annual meeting of the American Sociological

Association. My part of the paper was a discussion of student politics in America. The ASA paper was the actual beginning of this book.

In addition, I owe a special debt of thanks to Seymour Martin Lipset. He made extensive comments on various drafts of chapters in this book. He also provided me with much useful empirical information on student activism. All of this was of definite significance to me in preparing the final draft of the manuscript.

Part of the way through the project I benefited from an interview with David Horowitz. Horowitz wrote what was probably the first book on the New Left in the early Sixties, and his comments on the relationship between the Old Left and the New Left were most illuminating.

I would also like to thank the Department of Sociology and the Graduate Division at the University of California, Berkeley for providing small research grants that helped defray various expenses on this project. One such grant was a USPHS Predoctoral Fellowship. More generally, I would like to express my appreciation to Marilyn MacGregor and the staff in the Department of Sociology at Berkeley for all of their help over the years. I especially want to thank Louise Ruggles, whose conscientiousness and thoughtfulness helped expedite many aspects of this project.

Similarly, I am most grateful for the excellent technical computer assistance provided by the Survey Research Center at U. C. Berkeley. The entire book is better because of the competence of Margaret Baker, Heidi Nebel, and Frank Many.

A person's intellectual development is invariably influenced by his or her family and social background. I am certainly no exception. My mother and father always provided the support and encouragement necessary for the development of intellectual interests. My brother David frequently raised questions and issues of sociological significance that required a response on my part. And my good friend Betty Lovejoy, beginning early in my life, always brought up issues of public concern, which served as the basis for many enjoyable debates. For these and other reasons, I think my family and social background provided a particularly good starting point for the development of sociological interests, and for this I am most grateful.

My own two children, Ann and Jeffrey, probably had more to do with this book than is typically the case. For much of the time I was writing it, my wife was working part-time as a researcher in public health and ecology at U. C. Berkeley's School of Public Health. As a result, I had two little "research assistants" to help with my academic chores. They always livened up the project.

Finally, those who know my wife Patsy realize the great emotional and intellectual importance she has been to me. We have shared a great many experiences over the years: graduate school, work, our children, and a rich family life in general. Our relationship has had many benefits to me, not the least of which is her important influence on my sociological thinking. In a very concrete sense, she kept me up on the latest research with regard to various issues in this book. She was always acquainted with the specific topics I was dealing with, and she consistently provided me with recent references, articles, and books on these topics. Also she skillfully prepared the Index. In addition, she read and made excellent comments on the entire manuscript. Her comments have made a decided improvement in the final draft. I feel most fortunate to have had such a personally and intellectually compatible person with me during this project. It is for these reasons that I dedicate this book to her.

Introduction

The decade of the 1960s in the United States will long be remembered for the student political protest movement. This movement, which took the public and most of the academic community by surprise, had a widespread impact on many individuals and institutions. Much as the previous decade of the 1950s was characterized by a general political apathy, the decade of the 1960s was characterized by political consciousness and political conflicts. The Sixties were much more like the Thirties than any other decade of this century. In the Thirties, there were intense student protests related to the deepening political-economic crises in Europe and the United States; in the Sixties, there was a similar pattern of student protests over such volatile issues as Vietnam, civil rights, and educational reform.

One of the most heated debates of the Sixties focused on the best way to explain these protests. Were the students genuine political radicals who adhered to a Marxist-oriented critique of American society? Were they educational reformers or civil rights reformers who saw imperfections in the system, but who also felt the system could be "saved" through internal reform? Were they members of a New Working Class of educated laborers who finally saw that they were exploited as much as the Old Working Class of industrial workers? Or were the students merely using the political arena to rebel against their parents? Specific theories of student activism developed with regard to these and other explantions of the protests.

The purpose of this book is to empirically examine various theories of student activism of the Sixties. Many attempts to explain activism have been quite ideological in nature and have presented evidence for a favored position and de-emphasized evidence supporting other theories. This book gives a more balanced empirical test to many of the major theories of activism. By examining various theories, we hope to show the strength of our own approach to activism as well as the limits of other approaches. Actually, we argue that two theories—one middle-range and the other more general—are the most adequate explanations of activism in the Sixties.

Some of the specific theories to be examined here focus on the family, educational discontents, the development of a new working class of educated laborers in an advanced capitalist society, the role of civil rights ideology, the role of cultural alienation, the role of social alienation, and finally, a general theory of collective behavior will be used to analyze activism.[1] Some of the theories focus on the role of radical political consciousness in generating student activism (e.g., the family approach that emphasizes the continuity in radical ideology between activists and their parents). Other theories focus on the role of reformist political consciousness in generating activism (e.g., the approaches centering on the educational or civil rights ideology of activists). Another approach, that of the New Working Class, focuses on the combination of activists' critique of the educational system and the larger social system of corporate capitalism. We have called this type of ideology radical-reformist political consciousness.

In contrast to these approaches, which focus on some type of ideology of the activists, are the approaches to activism that de-emphasize the importance of ideology. Three such approaches are examined here. The most famous is the family conflict approach to activism. Instead of concentrating on the positive contribution of political consciousness in understanding activism, this approach sees activists taking out hostilities against their parents in the political arena. The two additional approaches considered here—cultural alienation and social alienation—also de-emphasize the role of political ideology in understanding participation in activism. The cultural alienation approach sees activists behaving in terms of distinct cultural values such as romanticism instead of explicitly political values; the social alienation approach focuses on the social malintegration and presumed loneliness of activists as central determinants of their political activities.

In presenting the evidence on these various approaches to student activism, we find strongest support for two approaches previously seen as incompatible. This evidence supports both the radical socilaization theory of activism and the family conflict approach. Two of the spokesmen for these positions—Richard Flacks and Lewis Feuer—have implied that their approaches are contradictory. Yet,we have found evidence for both theories. As a result, we suggest the following middle-range theory of student activism that synthesizes these otherwise opposite viewpoints: many activists act out radical political values that are derived from their parents' radical political or culturally unconventional values; yet the activists come into conflict with their parents because the activists feel the parents have not lived up to their own political or cultural values.[2] This type of position stresses the *ambivalence* in the relationship between activists and their parents; activists can agree with and act upon parental values, but these same values can serve as the basis of the conflict between the generations. However, once the student participates in activism, relations between the generations *improve*. This further suggests that activists often act out values derived from their parents.

In addition to establishing our middle-range theory of activism, in the final chapter we also argue that it is necessary to use a broad theory of collective behavior to more fully understand the development of activism in the Sixties. We synthesize Smelser's two main theoretical discussions of collective behavior into a general social-psychological model of collective behavior. This model is then used to broadly interpret the development of the student protest movement of the Sixties. It incorporates findings relative to the approaches that both emphasize and de-emphasize political ideology in understanding activism. In addition, it forces attention on other variables, such as structural conduciveness and structural strain, which are important to include in a fuller explanation of the political events of the Sixties. Thus, we combine the strengths of middle-range interpretations of activism with a broader theory of collective behavior to understand the political protests of the past decade. Furthermore, we use the same theory of collective behavior to give an interpretation to the *decline* of student activism by 1973. Finally, we use this theory of collective behavior to suggest conditions for the future renewal of activism in the United States.

Throughout this book, we refer to various studies of student activism. These studies occurred at different times and on different campuses throughout the United States in the Sixties. However, the main body of empirical findings are our own empirical data of the University of California, Berkeley campus, originally collected by Robert H. Somers and his methodology students and by Jeanne Block. These data were collected in 1968 and include both student and parental questionnaires, and a parental Q-Sort. Although much of the data concerns U. C. Berkeley, our theoretical and empirical focus is the United States. Especially in the last chapter we attempt to put various findings about student activism into a broader theoretical perspective than is typical in the literature on activism.

In the first chapter, we present an overview of the development of the New Left student movement in the Sixties. Then the following chapter outlines our own middle-range theory of activism. Qualitative evidence is presented in this chapter in support of our theory, and later chapters provide quantitative support. Chapter 3 presents a detailed analysis of a major type of ideology found among activists in the late Sixties, which is the period when our own quantitative data were collected. After the third chapter, the focus of the book becomes quantitative, and many theories of activism are tested. A methodology chapter outlining our rationale for testing these theories precedes the actual examination of the theories. Finally, the last chapter draws on the various empirical findings, as well as on Smelser's theory of collective behavior, to give a broad interpretation to the development, decline, and renewal of activism in the United States.

Notes

1. Elsewhere we have shown that each of these theories has a distinct position on the effect of political ideology on student activism, see James L. Wood, *Political Consciousness and Student Activism* (Beverly Hills: Sage Publications, in press).

2. As we will see, Kenneth Keniston is closest to our own middle-range position on student activism among the current commentators on the topic. However, there are important differences between his position and ours.

1

The Development of Student Activism in the United States

Participation in Student Protests

The earliest date of New Left student activism in the United States is probably 1957.[1] Amidst a good deal of political apathy and conservatism in the 1950s, there were some students actively concerned about civil rights, peace, free speech, and capital punishment. From these very modest beginnings in the late Fifties, there developed a more organized, viable student movement in the Sixties. In this chapter, we discuss the increasing participation in the New Left student movement throughout the Sixties and also indicate the increasing tendency toward radicalization in the movement.

Although the dominant political tone for students in the Fifties was conservative or apathetic, Altbach documents the existence of some liberal and even radical students throughout that decade.[2] In fact, he presents a convincing case for the view that the activism of the Sixties would not have occurred without the leftist political foundations of the Fifties.[3] In 1957, the first New Left political organization, SLATE, was founded at the University of California, Berkeley.[4] Also Altbach notes that "Socialist students were particularly involved in civil rights activities and instrumental in early mass demonstrations such as the Youth March for Integrated School in 1957 and 1958 and the early Freedom Rides and sit-ins.''[5] Thus, at Berkeley and at a few other campuses in the late Fifties there were the stirrings of discontent that would later develop into a full-fledged social movement.[6]

It was not, however, until February 1, 1960, that a distinct *student* movement emerged. The New Student Left actually began when Negro students sat in at segreqated lunch counters at Greensboro, North Carolina, on that date. Within a short time, many white students joined the Civil Rights Movement. A number of students came from the north and joined such organizations as SNCC (Student Non-Violent Coordinating Committee) and CORE (Congress of Racial Equality). The New Left is usually associated with white student radicals, but the first students to gain a national recognition for student protests were the Negro college students at Greensboro.

Although students were involved in civil rights protests dating from the Fifties, these were generally *off-campus* protests. The Berkeley campus was quite atypical in having student political protests *on* campus in the late

1

1950s. The Berkeley campus, in addition to its concern over civil rights, was also involved in campus protests over peace, capital punishment, and free speech prior to the Sixties. But it was not until the Free Speech Movement at Berkeley in 1964 that the protest movement in general began to center on the campus.

In fact, one could argue that the "white" student branch of the New Left did not emerge as an independent force until the Free Speech Movement, which occurred four years after the Greensboro sit-in. Although the FSM developed as a result of the university administration's refusal to permit solicitation of civil rights funds on the Berkeley campus, the civil rights issue soon drifted into the background. This time white students were fighting for their own rights and privileges, not for those of American Negroes. Until then, students had fought primarily for Negro justice. But after the FSM, white students became a political force differentiated from the Civil Rights Movement.

After the FSM there was a rash of student protests, both white and Third World, throughout the country. Protests eventually occurred on such divergent campuses as Harvard, University of California at Berkeley, University of Miami, Merritt College in Oakland, Howard University and the University of Colorado. Although civil rights and the Vietnam War were probably the two central issues of the New Left movement, protests also occurred at many schools over such issues as freedom of speech and assembly, living arrangements, classified research on campus, the multiversity's bureaucratic treatment of students, student power issues, such as student participation in faculty hiring, and the like.[7]

At U. C. Berkeley alone there were political activities such as the anti-Vietnam War march to the Oakland Army Terminal in 1965; the formation of the Vietnam Day Committee; and the 1966 Student Strike over naval recruiters on campus. In addition, there were unauthorized "teach-ins" over Vietnam; the 1967 Oakland Induction Center demonstrations; and the Third World Strike in 1968-69. Similarly, Berkeley experienced the People's Park protests in 1969; the protests, strike, and subsequent restructuring of the university over the Cambodian invasion in 1970; and the short-lived protests over Laos in 1971 and North Vietnam in 1972. These are only some of the more highly publicized examples of student activism at Berkeley. There were many other protests related to Vietnam, civil rights, student power, rights of university employees, and so forth.

The reason that all of these different protests can be considered in the same discussion is because of the rather broad definition of student activism. Student political activism is generally defined as the engagement by students in non-institutionalized political activities, such as illegal demonstrations against the Vietnam War, illegal civil rights protests, strikes, sit-ins, and other similar activities. This form of political activity is to be distinguished from institutionalized political activity of students, such as student government. Although it is possible to argue that demonstrations and related activities became institutionalized within the sub-culture of certain students, these activities were not institutionalized for society as a whole, which is the reference of this definition.

As the Sixties progressed, there were increasing numbers of students involved in this national protest movement, which culminated in the widespread protests over the Cambodian invasion in 1970. As early as 1964-65, Peterson reports protests over several issues at many colleges in the wake of the Free Speech Movement.[8] In 1966, U. C. Berkeley was the scene of the previously mentioned student strike in protest over the university permitting the navy to recruit on campus; this was, of course, part of the more general protest over the Vietnam War. This particular protest focused national attention on the relationship of the university to various "Establishment" institutions such as the military. In fact, within a month after the strike at Berkeley, there were many other similar protests throughout the country involving military, CIA, and Dow Chemical recruiters.[9]

By 1967-68, it was estimated that approximately 10 percent of the national student population was "capable of temporary activation depending on the issues."[10] Our own data on student activism at U.C. Berkeley, covering the period of 1964 to 1968, indicate that between 15 percent and 25 percent of the student body took part in major demonstrations, depending on the issues. (However, the overall trend at Berkeley is rather complex and is discussed in Chapter 9.)

By 1969, 292 major student protests took place on 232 college and university campuses in the first six months of that year.[11] A 1969 study of disciplinary measures on 28 campuses showed that more than 900 students had been expelled or suspended and that more than 850 students had been reprimanded.[12] The late FBI director J. Edgar Hoover reported that protests led to over 4,000 arrests during the 1968-69 academic year and about 7,200 arrests during 1969-70.[13]

The political protest movement reached its peak with the widespread protests over Cambodia in 1970. About 20 percent of the nation's colleges were on strike because of Cambodia, and the Urban Research Corporation reported that nearly one-third had some kind of protest.[14] The Student Strike Information Center at Brandeis University stated that 440 four-year colleges were on strike at least temporarily, and 286 colleges were on strike indefinitely over Cambodia.[15] Close to 80 percent of the nation's most academically selective schools had some kind of protest, and 9 percent of these schools even had violent demonstrations over Cambodia.[16] Drawing on survey data, Lipset estimates that almost half (49 percent) of the U.S. student population participated in some kind of protest related to Cambodia.[17]

4

In sum, there was a steady increase of student protest throughout the 1960s and into early part of the 1970s. In the late 1950s the New Left was only in its infancy, but a decade later there was widespread student protest over major government policies. Lipset presents longitudinal data that underscore this increasing tendency toward involvement in protests. On one hand, he shows that the precent of schools that reported incidents of activism at four time periods between 1967 and 1970 increased from 6.1 percent to 10.8 percent to 14.0 percent to 32.4 percent.[18] But even more spectacular is the increase in proportion of students involved in the protest movement over time. Drawing on data from the Harris Survey, Lipset shows that from 1965 to 1969 to 1970 the proportion of students who were involved in some kind of demonstration increased from 29 percent to 40 percent to a surprising 60 percent of the U.S. student population.[19] This means that by 1970 well over the majority of the U.S. student population had participated in at least some type of political protest. Of course, not all student protesters participated in illegal activities. This was especially the case during Cambodia when many people engaged in milder forms of protest than had been witnessed in prior demonstrations. By 1973, the campuses became a good deal quieter, but it should be clear that the New Left attracted a wide variety of students before it began to wane.

The Rise of Radical Political Consciousness

Along with the tendency of the movement to increase in numbers through-out the Sixties, there was also a tendency toward increasing radical ideology in the movement. In the early phase of the movement—approximately 1960 to 1964—a non-ideological tendency, along with a reformist tendency, prevailed, and even though there was a minority radical position in this early phase, it was not dominant. However, as the decade progressed, especially from 1965 to the early 1970s, the ideological tone of the movement did become more radical. It can thus be argued that the New Left combined a non-ideological tendency with tendencies to develop radical, reformist, and radical-reformist, left-wing ideologies. Here we spell out some of the general components of New Left ideology and also indicate some important changes in the ideology of the New Left as the decade of the 1960s developed.[20]

The New Left has often been called a non-ideological political movement by its supporters and detractors alike. This was especially the case with regard to the early phase of the movement. Some commentators have even argued that the New Left was antagonistic to any form of ideology, left-wing or right-wing. Frequently these commentators had in mind as a comparison the Communist Party, U.S.A., which, of course, was once a strongly ideological movement in the United States. The Communist Party had both positive and negative aspects to its ideology; it was against the entirety of capitalist society and it favored the establishment of a communist society along the lines of Russia. The early phase of the New Left did not have as many clearly defimed sources of enemies, and it did not offer a radical socialist or communist alternative to the existing liberal capitalist society of the United States. In fact, such documents as "The Port Huron Statement" of the Students for a Democratic Soceity (SDS) expressed a definite hesitation about "sure formulas" of social change.[21] In sum, the early phase of the New Left did not launch a radical critique of the existing capitalist system, nor did it propose radical alternatives to the system. As a result, the New Left in the early 1960s was considered non-ideological.

When the New Left is deemed non-ideological, this does not usually refer to *reformist* ideologies. Many of those in the early New Left were highly attached to reformist ideologies concerning civil rights for Negroes. The New Left, which actually grew out of the Martin Luther King-led Civil Rights Movement, was originally a reformist movement with goals such as increasing freedom and equality for Negroes within the existing social system.[22] (The New Left was, in addition, partly reacting against the Old Left by adopting a reformist position.[23]) While the early emphasis on participatory democracy—involvement of the poor and blacks in decisions that affected them as groups—was not radical ideology, it was a commitment to some type of ideology. These were all early efforts to generate change within the existing social system and thus reflected reformist views. In the year 1964, another reformist issue—free speech—launched one of the most famous student protests of the Sixties. The Free Speech Movement at U.C. Berkeley developed critiques against restrictions on speech, as well as more general educational criticisms, that were reformist in nature but not radical like those that attack capitalism, racism, and imperialism. Thus, in the early phase of the New Left, a reformist tendency clearly existed—along with the well-publicized non-ideological tendency. At this time, there was a hesitancy about radical ideology, but there was also a positive affirmation of various reformist ideologies.

The shift in at least part of the New Left to a more radical ideological position by the latter part of the Sixties is reflected in the increasingly radical tone of the literature of the late 1960s.[24] It is also reflected in interviews with activists of the late 1960s to be presented in the next two chapters. It is similarly reflected in the large body of quantitative data to be presented throughout the rest of this book. These quantitative data were collected in the latter part of the 1960s (i.e., in 1968) and are therefore a good indication of ideological tendencies of this period of the New Left. By 1968, these quantitative data show a higher relationship between radical political consciousness and student activism than between reformist political consciousness and student activism. In fact, by 1968 at Berkeley, one aspect of reformist consciousness—civil rights ideology—showed a moderate *negative* relation to student activism. Thus, there are important evidences of this shift to a more radical position in the New Left as the Sixties developed.

This increasing radicalism in the New Left was more of a "negative" or critical type than a "positive" variety of radical ideology. Smelser notes that the ideologies of protest movements—whether radical or reformist in nature—"have both negative and positive components."[25] "On the negative side there is a sense of foreboding, of great anxiety about threats to social life, and the specification of agents in society who are responsible for these threats."[26] In contrast, Smelser notes that "On the *positive* side, those who adhere to protest movements often endow themselves and the envisioned reconstitution of society with enormous power, conceived as the ability to overcome the array of threats and obstacles which constitute the negative side of the adherents' world-picture."[27] It is our contention that the negative aspects of radical ideology became more prominent in the New Left as the 1960s progressed; however, the commitment to specific socialist, communist, anarchist, or other more positive radical ideologies was weak throughout the decade.

There have been some recent calls for the development of socialist programs in what remains of the New Left.[28] These recent calls for socialist programs serve as further evidence of the *lack* of positive radical ideology in the New Left throughout the 1960s—if there were specific socialist programs to which activists were drawn in the Sixties, why is it now necessary to develop such programs?

In contrast to the lack of development of positive radical ideologies, the New Left eventually developed strong critiques of many U.S. social systems. Among the more prominent targets of a radical critique were the capitalist system, the imperialist system, the racist system, the power system, and the educational system. In a later chapter we will go into detail describing how New Left ideology was critical of these social systems. For example, many activists agreed with: (1) Marcuse's critique of U.S. corporate capitalism;[29] (2) Baran and Sweezy's attack on U.S. imperialism;[30] (3) Carmichael and Hamilton's Black Power critique of U.S. racism and internal colonialism;[31] (4) C. Wright Mills' attack on the undemocratic power system in the United States;[32] and (5) Herbert Gintis' attack on the U.S. educational system being linked to corporate capitalism.[33] Although not every author mentioned here would consider himself a member of the New Left movement, their ideas (and similar ideas of other theorists) became part of the New Left ideology in the latter part of the 1960s.[34]

It should be clear from the preceding discussion that New Left ideology involved a radical critique of a variety of social systems, not just one or two systems. This multiple critique partly distinguishes the New Left's radical ideology from the Old Left's radical ideology that primarily focused on the role of capitalism generating many problems. The New Left certainly attacked capitalism by the late 1960s, but the attack on capitalism did not exhaust the critique. In the empirical chapters to follow, the operational definition of the concept "radical political consciousness" reflects the various negative aspects of radicalism along with the goals of freedom and equality for submerged groups (see Appendix C).

A mixed type of political consciousness began to emerge in the student movement a few years after the Free Speech movement in 1964. At first glance, some of the critiques seemed like the educational critiques that existed ever since the FSM. But the new critique combined a radical criticism of capitalism with both negative criticisms of the educational system and more positive suggestions about educational reform. We call this radical-reformist political consciousness, and it is associated with the theory of the New Working Class to be discussed in Chapter 12.[35]

Thus, the New Left student movement began in the late Fifties with a close tie to the Civil Rights Movement. By the mid-Sixties it had become an independent political force that attracted more and more students and began to emphasize radical than reformist ideology. The question that arises in view of the evidence of such increased activism is: How can we explain the widespread participation in student protests of the Sixties? The next chapter outlines our particular middle-range theory of activism that attempts to answer this question.

Notes

1. Philip G. Altbach, *Student Politics in America* (New York: McGraw-Hill Book Company, 1974), pp. 119, 152; and Max Heirich and Sam Kaplan, "Yesterday's Discord," in Seymour Martin Lipset and Sheldon S. Wolin, eds., *The Berkeley Student Revolt* (Garden City, N.Y.: Anchor Books, 1965), p. 10.

2. Altbach, op. cit., Chapters Four, Five, Six, pp. 109-207. For an excellent discussion of the political apathy and conservatism of the 1950s, see Rose K. Goldsen, Morris Rosenberg, Robin M. Williams, Jr., and Edward A. Suchman, *What College Students Think* (Princeton, N.J.: D. Van Nostrand Co., 1960), p. 97.

3. Altbach, op. cit., pp. 203-5.

4. Ibid., p. 119.

5. Ibid., p. 152.

6. For an excellent discussion of political activism at Berkeley from the late Fifties to the early Sixties, see David Horowitz, *Student: The Political Activities of the Berkeley Students* (New York: Ballantine Books, 1962).

7. Richard E. Peterson, "The Scope of Organized Student Protest," in Julian Foster and Durward Long, eds., *Protest!: Student Activism in America* (New York: William Morrow & Co., p. 63, Table 1.

8. Ibid.

9. Jerome H. Skolnick, *The Politics of Protest* (New York: Ballantine Books, 1969), p. 98.

10. Peterson, op. cit., p. 78.

11. Urban Research Corporation, John Naisbitt, President, "Student Protests 1969," 5464 South Shore Drive, Chicago, Ill. 60615.

12. *Campus Unrest* (Washington, D.C.: U.S. Government Printing Office, 1970), p. 39.

13. Ibid.

14. Urban Research Corporation cited in *Campus Unrest,* ibid., p. 18.

15. *The Daily Californian,* The University of California, Berkeley, Vol. 206, No. 32, May 13, 1970, p. 1.

16. *San Francisco Chronicle,* "Top Colleges Had Strongest Reaction," October 3, 1970, p. 6.

17. Seymour Martin Lipset, *Rebellion in the University* (Boston: Little, Brown & Co., 1972), p. 90.

18. Ibid., p. 46.

19. Ibid., p. 45.

20. The present discussion is a highly condensed version of a much larger inquiry into the political consciousness of the New Left. For the larger discussion, see James L. Wood, *Political Consciousness as Reflected in the Literature of the New Left* (Beverly Hills: Sage Publications, Inc., forthcoming). The ideas discussed in this chapter form an important basis for the selection of specific items for the indices of some of the concepts in the quantative chapters of this book. The items are reported in Appendix C.

21. "The Port Huron Statement" of the Students for a Democratic Society (SDS), presented at the 1962 SDS Convention at Port Huron, Michigan, quoted in Paul Jacobs and Saul Landau, *The New Radicals* (New York: Random House, 1966), pp. 149-62.

22. For a discussion of New Left origins in the Civil Rights Movement, see Armand L. Mauss, "The Lost Promise of Reconciliation: New Left vs. Old Left," *The Journal of Social Issues* 27, No. 1 (1971): 12.

23. See Wood, op. cit.

24. For a discussion of New Left literature, see Ibid.

25. Neil J. Smelser, "Social and Psychological Dimensions of Collective Behavior," in his *Essays in Sociological Explanation* (Englewood Cliffs, N.J.: Prentice-Hall, 1968), Chapter Five, p. 116.

26. Ibid. Shils refers to the negative aspects of ideologies as "proto-ideological phenomena." See Edward Shils, "The Concept and Function of Ideology," *International Encyclopedia of the Social Sciences*, Vol. 7, p. 72.

27. Smelser, op. cit., p. 116.

28. Probably the first general meeting to discuss developing a socialist sociology was held in Denver, Colorado, at the 1971 national meeting of the American Sociological Association. See the Preliminary Program of the Annual Meeting of the American Sociological Association, Denver, Colorado, August 30 to September 2, 1971, Session 53, p. 36. The lead paper of this session was given by Richard Flacks and was published in *The Insurgent Sociologist*. See Richard Flacks, "Towards a Socialist Sociology: Some Proprosals for Work in the Coming Period," *The Insurgent Sociologist*, Vol. II, No. 2 (January-February 1972): 12-27. Subsequent meetings to discuss socialist sociology have been held at the 1972 meeting of the Pacific Sociological Association in Portland, Oregon, and at the 1972 meeting of the American Sociological Association in New Orleans, Louisiana. For a discussion of a democratic socialist movement arising out of the New Left, see Theirrie Cook and Michael P. Lerner, "The New American Movement," *Social Policy* 3 (July-August 1972): 27-31, 54-56. Lerner has recently written a book on the topic, *The New Socialist Revolution* (New York: Delacorte Press, 1973).

29. See Herbert Marcuse, *An Essay on Liberation* (Boston: Beacon Press, 1969).

30. See Paul A. Baran and Paul M. Sweezy, *Monopoly Capital* (New York: Monthly Review Press, 1966).

31. See Stokely Carmichael and Charles V. Hamilton, *Black Power: The Politics of Liberation in America* (New York: Vintage Books, 1967).

32. See C. Wright Mills, *The Power Elite* (New York: Oxford University Press, A Galaxy Book, 1956, 1965).

33. See Herbert Gintis, "The New Working Class and Revolutionary Youth," *Continuum* 8 (Spring-Summer 1970): 151-74.

34. Generally speaking, three types of people contributed to the ideology of the New Left: (a) student activists themselves; (b) older, white radical intellectuals; and (c) Third World intellectuals. For a discussion of these types of contributors to New Left ideology, see Carl Oglesby, "In-

troduction: The Idea of the New Left,'' in Carl Oglesby, ed., *The New Left Reader* (New York: Grove Press, 1969), pp. 1-20. For two excellent collections of essays on New Left ideology, see *The New Left Reader,* Ibid.; and Alexander Cockburn and Robin Blackburn, eds., *Student Power: Problems, Diagnosis, Action* (Baltimore: Penguin Books, in association with *New Left Review,* 1969).

35. For two discussions of this critique of both capitalism and the educational system, see Gintis, op. cit.; and John and Margaret Rowntree, ''The Political Economy of Youth: Youth as Class,'' published by *The Radical Education Project,* Box 625, Ann Arbor, Mich. 48107, pp. 1-36; it also appeared in *Our Generation,* Vol. 6, Nos. 1-2.

2 A Theory of Student Activism

The approach to understanding student activism that receives qualitative support in this chapter is that many student activists were responding to the political events of the past decade, such as the Vietnam War, in terms of the radical political values they acquired from their parents' distinctive political or cultural values. Stated differently, we feel that many student activists of the 1960s *acted out* radical political values derived from the process of unconventional family socialization. However, the activists also came into conflict with their parents because the activists felt the parents did not live up to their own political or cultural ideals.

Our middle-range theory of activism emphasizes the ambivalance in the relationship between activists and their parents. Furthermore, once the activists engaged in activism, this political behavior seemed to *improve* the relationship between the generations. This finding, in turn, adds indirect support to our theory that states positive links between parental values, student values, and activism. In sum, this model sees political and cultural values of the parents as important sources of student activism as well as sources of the conflict of generations. Yet the student's involvement in political conflicts tends to reduce the conflict between the generations because many students are acting out values to which their parents adhere.

Without the Civil Rights Movement the student movement would not have originated, and without the Vietnam War the student movement would not have reached the proportions it eventually did. The Civil Rights Movement created issues of moral concern over the many injustices to blacks in the United States. Flacks and others have shown that students from upper-status, politically left-wing, and culturally unconventional families were the main students who responded to the moral issues of civil rights in the first half of the 1960s.[1] Data of the late 1960s pointed to the role of Vietnam in broadening the social-economic base of the student movement.[2] The studies showed that by the late 1960s students from a variety of social-economic backgrounds participated in the movement instead of primarily upper-status students.[3] The studies suggested a variety of reasons for this broadening base of the New Left, but it is clear that the increasing involvement of the United States in Vietnam was of particular importance. In the last chapter of this book we will discuss in more detail the specific ways Vietnam was involved in developing the New Left.

Although the Vietnam War and the Civil Rights Movement were over-

arching sources of student protests, particular types of families were especially conducive sources of participation in the protests. As stated, the
social-ecnomic base of the movement had broadened by the late Sixties;
however, the political-cultural background of the activists remained distinctive even in the latter part of the decade. Our data of the late Sixties
indicate that many student activists did *act out* radical political values
derived from their parents' radical political or culturally unconventional
values.

With regard to parents who adhered to radical political ideology, we
argue that successful socialization to radical views occurred among many
student activists. The students, in turn, translated the radical ideology they
acquired from their parents into political activism in the face of the many
crises associated with civil rights and Vietnam. The argument is somewhat
more complex with regard to the association between unconventional
cultural views of the parents and student activism. We will argue in later
chapters that it was *not* the case that parents successfully socialized their
children to unconventional cultural values and that these *cultural* values
got translated into activism. This overly cultural approach to politics does
not receive much confirmation in our data. However, families that adhered
to unconventional cultural values seemed conducive to the development of
radical political consciousness in their children, and these radical political
views often got translated into activism. Our data clearly indicate two
parental sources of radical political consciousness and student activism:
(1) radical values of the parents and (2) unconventional cultural values of
the parents.

In a series of depth interviews, Keniston supplied interesting support
for the impact of parental values on student values and activism;[4] in turn,
our quantitative data support many of his views that are largely based on
qualitative data. In his study of anti-Vietnam activists, Keniston said that
"Especially for those from radical families, the process of radicalization
involves a return to the fundamental values of the family."[5] With regard to
this argument, he quotes an activist from a radical family:

Look, there never were any other values for me to make my own. . . . There were
always just clear lines between those values [of the rest of the community] and
mine, those of my parents. I could never adopt those, because they were always the
things that seemed opposed to me. Even if I had been a political dullard, from a
personal, ego point of view, I never could have done that. These are *my* values. In
college, I began to claim them as my own. They were no longer my family's,
because I had to defend them now on my own.[6]

Furthermore, according to Keniston, ". . . many of these young radicals
have identified themselves, from a very early age, with some tradition of
radical protest against injustice . . . [one radical] recalls in early childhood
attending with an admired relative a meeting of the editorial board of an Old

Left journal."[7] And another respondent in Keniston's study realized the impact of his family's left-wing values after involvement in the student movement:

You know, with all my background . . . I never really felt a part of it on my own until last year. . . . Then, for the first time, I really began to feel a part of the Movement . . . I began to be able to trace my own roots in terms of being able to feel actually *of* it, not only in it. . . . I saw that the type of work that was being done, the types of people that were being involved, and the goals that were being put forward—I began to feel that I was *of* these, that in terms of my background, that this was the thing *from which I had sprung*. That was a really good feeling. I began to feel, for the first time, that there was a kind of continuity in my whole political development. . . .[8]

Keniston also provides some support for our argument that parents adhering to culturally unconventional values tend to produce children with radical political values who engage in activism. In discussing the well-educated, affluent parents of many of his activists, he states: "Compared to their own parents, they are more likely to instill in their children the special values of self-actualization—independence, sensitivity to feelings, concern for others, free expression of emotion, openness, and spontaneity."[9] Furthermore, ". . . in some affluent families, one finds a parental devotion to the autonomy, self-determination, and dignity of children that is without precedent, even in American history."[10] In this book and elsewhere, Keniston sees a rather direct translation of these "special," or culturally unconventional values, into student activism, but our empirical data indicate *few* such direct links between cultural values of the parents, cultural values of the student, and student activism. On the other hand, Keniston hints at another avenue to activism with regard to the cultural values of the parents that is similar to our position. He seems to feel that political orientations of the student can emerge in culturally unconventional families and that the political values can get translated into activism.[11] Thus, he argues: "These are children, then, who have been taught from an early age to value independence, to think for themselves, to seek rational solutions, and to believe that principles should be practiced."[12] Keniston is not as explicit as we are on the links between the cultural values of the parents, radical ideology of the student, and student activism; but we hope to show the existence of these links in the quantitative data to be presented in later chapters.

Even though a continuity in values exists between activists and their parents, activists also tend to come into conflict with their parents. Many prior investigators have indicated that an approach stressing continuity between the generations is quite incompatible with an approach stressing conflict between the generations.[13] We feel these approaches are not incompatible. Although Pinkney does not emphasize the role of conflict in understanding student activism, he nevertheless presents qualitative evidence of family conflict for some of his civil rights activists. One respondent in his sample said:

I was a rebellious child and these factors were causing problems very early in my domestic life, even if I didn't wholly understand them.[14]

Another activist remarked:

My relationship with my parents was poor, characterized mostly by withdrawal to avoid abuse and conflict. My father was controlling, abusive, and my mother did little to protect me from this and attempted to inhibit any aggressive reaction of mine to my father's treatment . . .[15]

Still another activist in Pinkney's study said:

Mother—possessive, overprotective, smothering; Father—removed, cold, quick-tempered; Me—independent, secure, intellecutal.[16]

There is even limited evidence for a type of conflict Lewis Feuer was to emphasize, the Oedipal conflict. As one activist said:

In terms of sexual hang-ups, I think that's probably important, too. I don't know what it means, whether it's stronger in me or whether I was just more conscious of it, but without knowing the name of it, and without knowing it was a widespread thing, I was very conscious of the Oedipal thing. . . . I remember being very conscious of it and very distrubed by it. I don't remember consciously feeling anything in the least bit of antagonism toward my father at all. But I remember having definite fantasies about going to bed with my mother, and being very disturbed about them. . . . I would imagine that kind of thing must have been involved in my—I don't know.[17]

If the activist students are in so much ideological agreement with their parents, why then is there evidence of generational conflict? As suggested above, many activists come into conflict with their parents because the activists feel the parents have not lived up to their own political or cultural values—that is, student activists often feel their parents are hypocritical with regard to their own values. There were many problems for left-wing parents who were members of radical organizations during the McCarthy era of the Fifties; of course, some of these parents took part in political protests during the Thirties. Even if the activists could understand the inactivity of their ideological parents during a highly repressive era such as the McCarthy period, these same activists could not understand failure to enact left-wing or culturally unconventional values in a more politically permissive era such as the Sixties. These activists often saw their parents paying lip service to radical values, yet living middle-class, suburban existences nevertheless. Parental commitment to anything like full-time political activism was usually low in the Sixties, and the students saw this inactivity as being inconsistent with parental values. It is this perceived hypocrisy that generated various conflicts between the generations. As one activist stated:

From my father, I developed a sense that the present system was not legitimate, because he did not believe it was legitimate. . . . [My father] understood very clearly why people were exploited, and that that was terrible. That was one of the worst tragedies that could happen to somebody all of his life. . . . He also understood that business was a lot of fraud. . . . I'm sure my father has a much better understanding of what Stokely Carmichael is about than most people do . . . But his point of view would be a very narrow, selfish one. He would say [about the things that my friends and I are doing now]: "That's great, but let it happen after I'm dead. You guys can have your way then, but in the meantime I'm enjoying life."[18]

Clearly, this young radical admired his father's social-political values. But at the same time the son condemned the father for his refusal to take part in attempts to change the system, and he also condemned his father's desire to continue living a comfortable, middle-class existence. The son was decrying the hypocritical attitude his father did not even try to conceal.

With regard to activists from clearly radical backgrounds, there is even evidence of dialectical relations between continuity and conflict. For some, there appears to be continual struggle as the students move toward an independently radical position themselves. Thus,

Even [for the radicals] who come from radical families, their reconciliation with parental radicalism is far from complete, and it was accomplished only through inner conflict, turmoil, and outer rebellion. Indeed, these children of radicals were among those who rebelled *most* violently against their parents. And . . . though they accepted their parents' basic values, [they] rejected their parents' inactivity, ineffectuality, or acquiescence, together with many of the specifics of their formal political ideology.[19]

Again, we see evidence supporting our argument that family values are a source of activism *and* a source of generational conflict.

Other research using depth interviews has revealed statements of activists suggesting an agreement with parental values but a lament over parental failure to live up to their own political or cultural standards. An activist in Pinkney's sample stated:

[My parents] taught me to judge people as individuals without regard to "race," etc., but no longer do so themselves in practice.[20]

Another civil rights activist said: "Home was very religious and emphasized high moral standards—but standards of personal interaction were pretty low."[21] Examples could be multiplied, but the point is clear: acceptance by activists of parental values can co-exist with family conflict, and these values can serve to *generate* the conflict between the generations.

We are thus suggesting a middle-range theory of activism that emphasizes the *ambivalence* of the relationship between activists and their parents. In the most elaborate statement of the antagonisms between activists and their parents, Lewis Feuer's *The Conflict of Generations,* there is an emphasis on only one side of Freud's insights about parent-child relations.[22] This, of course, is the negative side. According to Feuer, student activists hate their parents and take this hatred out in the political arena by rebelling against political authority figures. But even in *Totem and Taboo,* Freud did not only emphasize the hatred of the sons for the father. He also stated that the sons admired and identified with the father.[23] In fact, throughout *Totem and Taboo*—a book Feuer cites in support of his conflict thesis—Freud again and again emphasizes the importance of the *ambivalences* the sons felt toward the father. We will develop this point in a later chapter; but here we wish to establish that our data point to rather complex and ambivalent relations between activists and their parents that are not entirely conflictual but are not entirely harmonious.

In-depth interviews with activists reveal some of the ambivalences of the parent-child relationship. Commenting on his relations with his father, one male activist said:

I used to have these long talks with my father when we went on walks—these strange kinds of long talks. In a way, it was my political education . . . he'd tell me sort of a child's version of working-class history, revolutionary history. I think it went through until I was eight or nine. . . . He would tell me about the origins of money and things like that. . . . He clearly went out of his way to do it.[24]

Yet for all the positive images of this father in teaching his left-wing political ideology, the same activist also remarked about his father:

My father, on the other hand, is sort of accommodating . . . [I tend to think] of my father as being non-masculine. And I tend to look in myself for traits of his . . .[25]

Similarly, we recall the activist whose father was unusually understanding of the plight of oppressed people, yet the son criticized him for wanting to live a most conventional middle-class existence. Still another activist was quite explicit on the topic: ". . . I alternated between love and hate for my parents; the usual thing, but more intensified."[26]

This ambivalence in the relationship between activists and their parents is accentuated for activists in relation to the parent of the same sex. One study found a split in parental image for almost all the activists interviewed when the activist was discussing the parent of the same sex.[27] Our own data indicate many of these same ambivalences. It was not until we took sex of the respondent into account that we actually uncovered a relationship between family conflict and student activism. However, the strong intensification of the ambivalences between activists and the parent of the same sex—with all of the Freudian overtones—receives only partial support in our data. Yet, evidence of this type of relation between the generations, as well as a good deal of ideological continuity, suggests ambivalence in the relationship between activists and their parents.

Once the student has engaged in activism, we found a rather unexpected result—namely, an *improvement* in the relations between the generations. This is quite contrary to what one would expect to find on the basis of reading much prior literature on activism.[28] Nevertheless, one of our stronger empirical findings suggests that family relations are improved when the student engages in activism. When the parents of activists were asked if the relationship with their children had recently improved, deteriorated, or remained the same, the largest proportion said relations with their activist children had recently improved. We took this finding as additional evidence that the students were indeed acting upon values derived from their parents. In fact, it has even been suggested that many parents of activists truly admire the fact that their children are enacting parental values.[29]

One reason that activism improves family relations may be that it opens channels of communication between the generations that were previously closed. The act of students engaging in anti-institutional behavior brings up questions of basic values. These issues could serve to facilitate communication between parents and their children, and the increased communication could indicate broad agreement on social-political issues between the generations. As one activist noted:

I think that participation in the civil rights movement has forced me to talk with my family much more than before. At first they were very opposed, but have modified their view since then. From this we have gained mutual understanding, and our relations are better now than they have been for six or seven years . . .[30]

In addition to improved communication, this activist suggested implicitly the role of reverse socialization in the families of some activists (i.e., the student socializes his parents to a more radical view than they originally held). Thus, student activism (and the adherence to radical ideology) seem to have more positive functions for the family than is usually thought to be the case.

When we argue that political values of the parents influence student activism, we refer specifically to *radical* values of the parents, not to *liberal* parental values. This is a position not often found in the analysis of activism in the literature. Usually radical and liberal values of the parents are blurred in the analysis of "left-wing" family orientations; or liberal values are explicitly seen as having the same effect as radical parental values.[31] Our data separated liberal from radical political orientations of both the parents and the students, and we feel that radical parental values are much more associated with activism than liberal parental values.

In general, radical political values refer to the actor's desire to obtain greater freedom and equality for submerged groups through making a change *of* the social system. Liberal political values also refer to the actor's desire to obtain greater freedom and equality for submerged groups, but by making changes *in* the social system. For example, a radical position on how to eliminate poverty would argue that poverty is a function of industrial capitalism; hence, capitalism must be abolished to end poverty. A reformist position would argue that it is not necessary to abolish capitalism to eliminate poverty; instead, changes within the capitalist system, such as changing the tax structure and increasing the minimum wage, would be sufficient to end poverty. Both the liberal and radical positions wish to see poverty ended; but the liberal view feels it can be done within the existing system whereas the radical view feels the system must be abolished first.

Much evidence in our study supports the links between radical political values of the parents, radical political values of the student, and student activism. In contrast, much weaker links exist between liberal political values of the parents, liberal political values of the student, and student activism. Similarly, only weak links exist between liberal political values of the parents, radical political values of the student, and student activism. Thus a liberal parental background is simply not as predictive of radical political consciousness and student activism as a radical parental background.

The implications of our findings on parental background and activism are that a *radical* socialization hypothesis is supported, but not a *liberal* socialization hypothesis. The radical ideology of the parents seems to get translated, through the socialization process, into radical ideology and activism of the students, but not liberal parental ideology. It is often stated that activists come from the same "left-wing" side of the political spectrum as their parents but that the activists are more radical than their parents.[32] This type of conclusion is *not* supported by our data, which indicate, instead, that activists and their parents *share* a radical ideology. Due to the importance of this point, we ran many tests of the liberal socialization hypothesis, but we came up with a series of negative results.

A situation where activists might well be more ideologically radical than their parents is the case of activists who derive their political views from their parents' unconventional *cultural* values. The reader will recall that our position is that a student's radical ideology and activism can be derived from unconventional cultural values of the parents as well as from radical political values of the parents. Many parents who hold unconventional cultural values undoubtedly also hold radical political values. But these are separate types of values, and a parent or student could be high on one set of values but low on the other set. Thus, if the source of student activism is the cultural orientations of the parents, then the student may well be more radical than the parents. But if the parent's political ideology is the source of a student's radical consciousness and activism, then we argue that the students are not more radical than their parents. Instead they all tend to share a radical political ideology.

When we refer to the radical ideology of the parents, this does not usually refer to Communist Party ideology. Although some of the parents in our sample may have been associated with the C.P. in their youth, our data indicate little parental association with radical political *organizations* like the Communist Party or various socialist parties.[33] Certainly there are well-publicized examples of truly "red-diaper baby" activists, but out data of "rank and file" activists indicate that the large majority of the parents belong to established political parties—either the Democratic or Republican Party. Among the parents who do belong to established political parties, there are some who nevertheless adhere to a radical political ideology. It is these parents, along with culturally unconventional parents, who are most likely to produce a radically conscious activist child.

Notes

1. Richard Flacks, "The Liberated Generation: An Exploration of the Roots of Student Protest," *The Journal of Social Issues* 23 (July 1967): 52-75. Also see Alphonso Pinkney, *The Committed: White Activists in the Civil Rights Movement* (New Haven: College and University Press, 1968). Pinkney does not emphasize the role of upper-status students in the Civil Rights Movement as do Flacks and others.

2. Milton Mankoff and Richard Flacks, "The Changing Social Base of the American Student Movement," *The Annals of The American Academy of Political and Social Science* 395 (May 1971): 54-67.

3. Ibid. Also data reported in this book indicate a broadening social-economic base of the student movement by the late 1960s.

4. Kenneth Keniston, *Young Radicals* (New York: Harcourt, Brace & World, 1968).

5. Ibid., p. 113.

6. Activist, cited in ibid.

7. Keniston, ibid., p. 119.

8. Activist, cited in ibid., p. 123.

9. Keniston, ibid., p. 245.

10. Ibid.

11. Ibid., p. 246.

12. Ibid.

13. See Flacks, op. cit.; and Lewis S. Feuer, *The Conflict of Generations* (New York: Basic Books, 1969). However, Keniston, op. cit., would disagree. Altbach calls for further research on the role of generational conflicts in activism, and we hope to provide some additional empirical material in this book; see Philip G. Altbach, "Student Activism and Academic Research: Action and Reaction," in Philip G. Altbach and David H. Kelly, *American Students: A Selected Bibliography on Student Activism and Related Topics* (Lexington, Mass.: Lexington Books, D.C. Heath, 1973), p. 22.

14. Activist, cited in Pinkney, op. cit., p. 56.

15. Ibid., p. 57.

16. Ibid.

17. Activist, cited in Keniston, op. cit., p. 80.

18. Ibid., pp. 58-59.

19. Keniston, ibid., p. 219.

20. Activist, cited in Pinkney, op. cit., p. 59.

21. Ibid.

22. Feuer, op. cit., p. 162.

23. Sigmund Freud, *Totem and Taboo,* Authorized Translation by James Strachey, (New York: W.W. Norton & Co., 1950), pp. 128-61.

24. Activist, cited in Keniston, op. cit., p. 57.

25. Ibid, pp. 57-58.

26. Activist, cited in Pinkney, op. cit., p. 57.

27. Keniston, op. cit., p. 55.

28. Especially see Feuer, op. cit., for an opposite expectation.

29. Kenneth Keniston, "The Sources of Student Dissent," in Neil J. Smelser and William T. Smelser, eds., *Personality and Social Systems,* Second Edition (New York: John Wiley and Sons, 1970), p. 686.

30. Activist, cited in Pinkney, op. cit., pp. 58-59.

31. Keniston, *Young Radicals,* op. cit., and Flacks, op. cit., seems to feel liberal parental values have the same effect as radical parental values. Lipset often blurs the two types of political ideologies when he uses the term "liberal-to-left" political ideology. See Seymour Martin Lipset, *Rebellion in the University* (Boston: Little, Brown & Co.), p. 83.

32. Ibid., p. 80.

33. For an interesting discussion of former parental membership in Old Left political organizations, see S. M. Lipset, "Student Opposition in the United States," *Government and Opposition* 1 No. 3 (April 1966): 369.

3

The Dimensions of Radical Political Consciousness

Introduction

Up to now the term radical political consciousness has been used in a rather abstract fashion to indicate the desire to obtain freedom and equality for submerged groups by making a change of the social system. Here, we further define this concept (which for us, is synonymous with radical political ideology)[1] and we cite statements made by activists that suggest many of them are attached to radical viewpoints.

The concept "change *of* the social system" refers to the large-scale rearrangement of the existing system.[2] The system involved could be a national social system like the United States, one of various "sub-systems"—such as the economic sub-system, the political sub-system, the race and ethnic sub-system—or the entire international system. Ideological statements by activists about making broad changes of these various systems and sub-systems are thus indicative of their radical political consciousness.

In particular, this chapter considers activists' critiques of capitalism, racism, imperialism, the university as part of the larger system, and the political system; and it examines their statements for commitments to radically alternative social systems to the existing capitalist system. These alternative systems include socialism and an anarchist society without the state or other forms of external regulation of individuals.

The various topics such as capitalism and racism are considered separately here, although all are aspects of a radical point of view. The New Left did not attempt to derive all social-political phenomena from capitalism, as did some branches of the Old Left. For example, racism and capitalism are discussed separately, not because there are no links between them, but because some activists in the New Left looked at racism as at least partially distinct from capitalism. Also, socialism was not seen by most New Left members as a single solution to all major problems. In particular, many in the New Left felt the issues of women's liberation and racism would still have to be dealt with even after a socialist victory. However, we are definitely interested in evidence concerning criticism by activists of the entirety of capitalist society in the United States and the call for its replacement by a radically different type of society that is felt would increase freedom and equality for submerged groups (e.g., a socialist society).

21

Capitalism

Although the New Left was not as quick to derive various social-political phenomena from capitalism as the Old Left, many in the New Left did view capitalism as the source of many problems.[3] Many activists saw capitalism as the source of racism, imperialism, poverty, and exploitation. In fact, it is often difficult to separate a discussion of capitalism from these specific issues, which are the context in which capitalism is criticized. Thus, the focus here is on activists' views of capitalism, but many other topics such as the university, racism, imperialism, and unequal distribution of power are also involved.

Capitalism refers to an economic system in which the means of production are privately owned instead of societally owned. Classically, a capitalist system involved a sharp division between the owners of the means of production and those who worked for the owners. Marx, of course, referred to this division as the separation between the bourgeoisie and the proletariat. With the advent of the modern corporation, there has been a change from smaller-scale private enterprise to large-scale corporate capitalism. Although there are important differences between classic capitalism and corporate capitalism, both forms nevertheless involve a smaller group of people owning the means of production and a larger group of wage earners who work for the owners. It is the capitalist system—in the classic form and especially in the modern form—that activists tend to oppose because they feel it leads to exploitation and domination of people in the United States and throughout the world.

Some typical New Left sentiments against the capitalist system are expressed in the activists' statements that follow. These statements are from unpublished studies of Berkeley students that were informed by my research on activism.

I believe I fit into the revolutionary political consciousness which gives rise to student activism. First and foremost, I came from a radical background and was socialized into an "anti-establishment" way of being. As I matured I found out that my parents *did* teach me correctly and that an oppressive, racist society does in fact exist. As a student I am fighting to change the university. In fact I almost feel that my attendance is a "cop out" and that by being a student I am merely doing what society wants me to do. But as long as I fight for change, as long as I view the university as a mere extension of the capitalist system, and as long as the final product is that of a revolutionary consciousness, I need not worry about being a student. . . . I believe that all students with a revolutionary consciousness are an extremely important asset to the left movement.

I would have to fit myself in with the radical category. I see no way of achieving equality under a capitalist system such as ours. . . . Our system has developed to "oligopolistic" capitalism with hundreds of corporations controlling things. The exploitation of people at home and around the world is so obvious one can only want to see its end. . . . The consumerism, poverty, failure of civil rights [reform] make people see that the values of our "leaders" are nowhere and their way of life is death.

This society is based on money. The evidence is that human life is worth less than the dollar. This society is based more on to each according to his ability than need, but really not according to ability either. To each according to his ability is one of the projected values, not real values. All potentials are stifled, and this is one of the important things in my concept of what the Third World should overcome.

[The] president and politicians are only tools, too. Like, if you offed the president we have now, and put in a new president, you'd still have the same society run by the same institutions, or whatever to deal with. Even if they ended the war in Vietnam, they would have to do the same thing, or the equivalent someplace else.

I was in Chicago during the SDS action of October 8 to 11, although I supported the RYM II [the Revolutionary Youth Movement II] faction as opposed to the Weatherman faction. I went to Washington for the November 15th March. . . . I suppose I would classify myself a radical in that I do not believe that Third World people or women will attain equal rights within a capitalistic system. I do not believe racism, chauvinism, imperialism or militarism will be dealt with within a reformist ideology.

Clearly, there is opposition to capitalism among these activists. They see capitalism in the United States promoting militarism, racism, and imperialism, as well as poverty, powerlessness, and political manipulation. These phenomena are looked at as decided evils by the activists, and they feel the proper remedy is not in reformist solutions but instead in the abolition of capitalism.

In our survey, there were only a few "open-ended" questions in which the activists had the opportunity to discuss capitalism in their own terms. Actually, there was not even one open-ended question that directly solicited the activists' opinions of capitalism *per se* although there were some "closed-ended" questions. It was mainly in the context of activists discussing U. C. Berkeley's ties to the larger society that the activists had a chance to discuss their views of capitalism. We can see evidence that Berkeley activists felt U. C. Berkeley was too closely tied to corporate capitalism; this, in turn, implies a criticism of the capitalist system by activists (i.e., if the activists approved of capitalism, they would not feel U. C. Berkeley was too closely tied to it).

Ever since Clark Kerr, former president of the University of California, announced that the university serves the existing social arrangements, radicals have used that same argument against the university.[4] Many have argued that the university in the United States is either "irrelevant" or relevant to the wrong purposes—that is, the university supports U.S. capitalism in particular and the "military-industrial complex" in general.

They see economic interests dictating university policy, and they are critical of the subservience of the university to the larger society.

For example, one activist in the study felt that the university's Board of Regents was "intimately related to [the] states' largest economic interests," while another believed: "[The university is too closely tied to established society because of] money—we have to get it from Reagan. [The] state has control over the 'U.' The state is controlled by monopolies, and powerful lobbies. Bourgeoisie Power." Still another student activist saw an "exchange relationship" between the economic system and the university: "[The] economic establishment pays for education and education must pay it back." One opinion gathered in the study indicated the tie between the university and established society is too close "because financial and other—more social [e.g., prestige]—rewards operate both on [the] university administration and on [the] faculty members." In particular, said one activist, "[Look at] the University's, e.g., engineering's, connections with [the] war industry . . .," and according to another:

Examine [the] composition of [the] Board of Regents—business, large military aircraft corporations, and other reactionary forces in the state. Over 50 percent of [the] budget for [the] University comes from [the] Defense Department.

In sum, there is evidence that various student activists oppose U.S. capitalism. The more quantitative nature of the association between opposition to capitalism and student activism will be explored in another chapter since antagonism to capitalism is part of the index of radical political consciousness.

Imperialism

More than any other issue, the Vietnam War brought up the idea that the United States was an imperialist country. Although there are various definitions, imperialism usually refers to some form of domination by one country over the economic, political, and military affairs of another country. There have been many interpretations of why the United States got involved in Vietnam, and these interpretations range from the charge of imperialism to the justification of the U.S. "defense of liberty" in Vietnam. Similarly, there have been numerous versions of the imperialist theory of U.S. involvement in Vietnam among those who adhere to this overall position.

Some of the variations on the theme of imperialism argue that the United States was involved in Vietnam: (1) to prevent a communist encroachment in Southeast Asia, which the government feels would eventually damage U.S. overseas economic investments; (2) to exploit minerals and oil in Southeast Asia, which would not be possible if the Communists took over in Vietnam and elsewhere; and (3) to prevent the "domino theory" from working out in practice (i.e., the United States must prevent a communist takeover in Vietnam to prevent similar takeovers throughout Asia, if not a wider area).[5] All of these theories emphasize that the United States gains in a political-economic way by remaining in Vietnam.

While imperialism is often discussed in the same breath as capitalism, the topics are distinct. Imperialism is conceived of as a system of relationships between whole nations and can therefore be supported or opposed as a system. Hence, an opposition to imperialism as a social system would be, as we have defined it, another instance of radical political consciousness.

The quantitative data to be discussed in later chapters contain at least some general items on students' ideological oppostion to U.S. involvement in Vietnam. The qualitative data presented here indicate activists' opposition to Vietnam as part of their opposition to U.S. imperialism. Various activists have stated:

[I favor a] victory of the Viet Cong. The war [is a] logical extension of American foreign policy [which is] disastrous. [The war is] probably [the] most disastrous event in U.S. history and the country will undergo revolutionary changes in large part because of the war.

[The] U.S. government is beginning to react [to the] whole world like they treat [people in] Vietnam.

The main reason we are there is not because of Communists, but because of the minerals that are there [i.e., tin].

[Vietnam will be] remembered by as much shame as [the] Spanish-American War or [the] Marine action in [the] Western Hemisphere in [the] early twentieth century.

[I] disagree [with the U.S. having a "moral commitment" to Vietnam if this means] SEATO/communism stuff.

[The] U.S. war effort [is] entrenched politically and economically—[it makes a] mockery of a moral obligation to [the Vietnamese] people.

Some activists directly advocated non-participation in the war for themselves and others: "We should get out this very afternoon. I'm not going —absolutely not—[I] will leave this country before I'll go." "[I] advocate active resistence [to the Vietnam war]." And the familiar slogan, "Get out of Vietnam. Hell No, We Won't Go," was echoed by another activist.

Two other studies of Berkeley students that were informed by this research on activism similarly indicate anti-imperialist sentiments among student activists. One activist stated:

I think our racist arrogance deluded us into thinking we could use our customary devices of buying off enough greedy Vietnamese lackeys so that we could freely exploit the labor and resources of the country while at the same time secure an army to stave off the surrounding Communists. As it turned out, there were enough Vietnamese people who were aware of the history of Western imperialism and its affects on their homeland. Their resistence invited further military attention from us, of course. . . .

The same activist continues later in the interview:

The fact that they want money ties in. Like they try to rip off as many material resources as they can overseas in order to increase their potential for cornering the market on all kinds of stuff. They do the same thing at home in terms of labor by exploiting Third World people by making them work at cheap wages. Besides the economic exploitation, their racist attitudes are tied together. They're racist toward blacks, brown people, and Asians abroad and at home . . . the ghettoes in the states are colonialist, so another form of imperialism. The same attitudes are involved.

These anti-imperialist views are basically similar to those of the critics of capitalism who argued that imperialism cannot be dealt with through reformist ideology, that purely political solutions to wars like Vietnam are futile, and that the United States has developed into an ''oligopolistic'' capitalist system that exploits on a worldwide scale. Thus, as was the case with capitalism, there is qualitative evidence that various student activists oppose U.S. imperialism, especially with regard to U.S. involvement in Vietnam.

Racism

Another focus of the radical critique of American society centers on racism. Racisim can be looked at as an individual phenomenon, and it can be viewed as an institutional phenomenon. As Carmichael and Hamilton point out:

Racism is both overt and covert. It takes two, closely related forms: individual whites acting against individual blacks, and acts by the total white community against the black community. We call these individual racism and institutional racism.[6]

Furthermore, Carmichael and Hamilton argue that institutional racism is colonialism and that black people are colonial subjects within the United States—that is, they feel black people are controlled politically, economically, and socially by an external force: white society. As a result, they condemn the entire social system of the United States as a racist system, and they call for the development of new institutions.[7]

They offer the concept of Black Power as a solution to the problems of racism and internal colonialism. Interestingly enough, there is a radical and reformist aspect to the strategy of Black Power. The component referring to the illegitimacy of the entire racist system and the parallel demand for new institutions is radical. In contrast, the idea that Black Power is the latest type of ethnic power to be used for economic and political advantage in American society (similar to the Irish, Jews, and Italians) is not very different from the reformist approach of Glazer and Moynihan in *Beyond the Melting Pot*.[8] However, the important point for our purposes is that the Black Power movement is associated with a radical critique of the entire racist social system in the United States. As will be seen in our quantitative data, reformist civil rights ideology has a negative association with student activism, but the more radical Black Power ideology has a strong positive association with activism.

The qualitative evidence in my study indicates that activists, including white activists, endorse calls for Black Power and an end to the racist system, a view which is supported by the data cited here from other studies informed by our research on activism. As will be noted, the issue of racism for many activists comes up in the context of other issues such as Vietnam. This means that various activists connect the different elements of the radical critique of American society into a rather broad condemnation of the United States as a total system. Some of the anti-racist sentiments are as follows:

. . . you have to have Vietnamization in Vietnam so you can have war in Laos. . . . Racism kind of goes along with it. To detract from racism at home you carry it on abroad . . .

The war [in Vietnam] reflects the disregard for individuals—killing of Vietnamese doesn't matter—[the] same thing [happens] in the U.S. with [the] treatment of minorities.

I began to understand peoples' support of the Panthers and violent solutions. I felt a constant inner conflict between my desire for the end of racism, and my actions which were limited to only a couple of Free Huey rallies.

[When I was younger] I didn't really have an awareness of class conflict. I read Marx in high school, but I could barely understand what he was talking about. I would say, though, that what I had personally experienced as racism I translated into political thought. So that had a good deal of effect on my political consciousness.

Thus, opposition to racism is different than the more limited opposition to prejudice and discrimination against minorities; opposition to racism focuses on entire systems of relationships, not just on individual attitudes and behavior.

Unequal Distribution of Power

Highly influenced by C. Wright Mills' *The Power Elite,* many student activists came to criticize the existing system of power in the United States.[9] Mills argues that those in the "command posts" of the three major institutions of American society—the government, industry, and the military—make decisions that mightly affect large numbers of U.S. citizens, as well as people throughout the world. The vast majority of people do not control decisions that are made for them by the power elite; and these decisions have the most serious consequences for the masses of people in the United States, as well as the international masses. In sum, Mills launched a major attack on the power system in the United States, holding that this unequal distribution of power meant the United States was not a democratic society.

There is solid evidence that many activists perceive an unequal distribution of power in the United States. They feel that ordinary men and women, including themselves, do not control their own destinies and that elites do make decisions that have serious consequences for them. They feel this system of power distribution is undemocratic and that it should be replaced with a system in which power is more equally distributed.

Furthermore, some activists not only see the distribution of power in Mills' terms, but they see worse effects than he predicted. In particular, some activists not only see unequal distribution of power in American society, but they see the rise of fascism as a distinct possibility in America. They think that "it could happen here." One activist in the study felt that if the Vietnam War "continues at its present pace or is escalated, then it will eventually create a fascist dictatorship in the United States." Similarly, another activist stated:

[Social problems can be solved] in two ways. Annihilation of the institutions, systems, structures, procedures, etc. . . . like schools, etc., things that are holding back people's potential, stopping people from expressing themselves, stopping people from asking questions. That's one of the most important things about the fascism problem; people aren't asking questions enough, because when they ask questions they get stung. The practical aspect is revolution, and the beginning part of that is self-defense. We have to defend our own minds, and also our bodies.

Still other activists said that the United States is an "oppressive society."

It is important to consider at this point one of the most persistent demands in the student movement (as well as in Third World communities):

the demand to "control one's own destiny." This demand flows directly from Mills' arguments about the lack of control over decisions and lack of involvement in the processes of decisions by the large majority of people. The early Port Huron Statement of the Students for a Democratic Society states:

Although mankind desperately needs revolutionary leadership, America rests in national stalemate, its goals ambiguous and tradition bound instead of informed and clear, its democratic system apathetic and manipulated rather than "of, by, and for the people."[10]

Similarly,

We would replace power rooted in possession, privilege, or circumstance by power and uniqueness rooted in love, reflectiveness, reason, and creativity. As a *social system* we seek the establishment of a democracy of individual participation, governed by two central aims: that the individual share in those social decisions determining the quality and direction of his life; that society be organized to encourage independence in men and provide the media for their common participation.[11]

This call for "participatory democracy" was elaborated in various forms throughout the Sixties; in fact an important publication of the movement was given a title indicating concern with the problem of control and liberation in American society (*Leviathan*). Scott and Lyman, in their review of New Left ideology, sum up this concern with freedom and control:

Throughout the current movement we hear demands for personal freedom, group independence, and general liberation from legal restraints, customary controls, and social inhibitions. The belief system here is the obverse side of the theme of powerlessness. Men are impotent to influence public policy or personal life under current arrangements. As a result, political life is perceived as oppressive. Citizens are effectively enjoined from their civic opportunities at the same time that they are reminded of their patriotic duties. . . . Autonomy promises a fundamental shift in the political arrangements among men. . . . Men will recover their lost power to challenge fate, control destiny, and manage affairs. Instead of one or several oligarchical power elites controlling human action, power itself will become diffused and distributed over mankind in general so that each individual senses his own mastery over his own life. . . . Man will be able to do, think, and act as he pleases, unfettered by rules, roles, or regulations.[12]

Students in the movement, as well as theorists such as Marcuse, have voiced a concern about the goal of freedom in modern society. We have seen evidence that many activists agree with Mills that elites make decisions for the majority of people in American society, and as a result most people do not have a great deal of influence over important decisions that affect them. Further empirical analysis of this topic will be conducted in a later chapter since perceived powerlessness is part of the concept of radical political consciousness.

Socialism

Up to this point, we have primarily discussed what the New Left is "against"—that is, many members of the New Left are against capitalism, imperialism, racism, and power structures. The next two sections focus on what the New Left is "for"—that is, many activists' have expressed interest in socialism as well as in anarchism. Both a socialist society and an anarchist society are types of society that can be considered radical alternatives to the existing corporate capitalist society in the U.S.

There is some evidence of a socialist commitment in the New Left. A socialist commitment would refer to the individual's support of some form of societal ownership of the means of production. There are, of course, many varieties of socialism that range from the state's ownership of a few industries, to state ownership of all major industries, to workers' control of the means of production, to the abolition of most or all bases of stratification and allocation of privileges. These are only a few very broad socialist possibilities that by no means exhaust the limitless faction fights that can occur within and between various socialist parties.

The evidence of a socialist commitment in the New Left usually involves student activists stating on a questionnaire that they are socialists rather than Democrats or Republicans. For example, Pinkney found that the modal political response among his civil rights activists was socialist rather than Republican or Democrat.[13] Similarly, an early analysis of our data indicated that student activists were more likely to report a socialist political affiliation than affiliation with the Democratic or Republican parties.[14] In addition, the activists in our study tended to support government ownership of industries, which is one form of socialist orientation.

There are other studies and assessments of the student movement that bear on the issue of socialism in the New Left. In addition to Pinkney's and this study, Flacks, Horn and Knott, Lyonns, and Miller have presented empirical data on a socialist commitment among some student activists.[15] For example, Miller found that self-proclaimed revolutionaries among the protestors at the 1968 Democratic National Convention in Chicago were more likely than non-revolutionaries to "support (non-authoritarian) communism."[16] Also, Flacks presents data indicating socialist views on the part of many activists.[17] And Oglesby lists four "basic positions on the identity of the New Left," one of which is a socialist position involving students and workers that he feels is "the most familiarly radical position."[18] Finally, it might be noted that some former student activists, now Professors of Sociology (and this includes Richard Flacks), have organized sessions at the Pacific Sociological Association and American Sociological Association on developing a "socialist sociology."[19]

It is perhaps this last bit of evidence on the socialist commitment among student activists that indicates the weakness of the argument. If the socialist commitment were so strong among student activists, why, at this late stage of the game, is it necessary to organize meetings to develop a socialist perspective among activists and former student activists? The reason is that various members of the New Left may have certain socialist leanings, but the New Left has not yet worked out anything like a comprehensive socialist position. It has not decided between the various possible socialist alternatives. Outside of tightly-knit revolutionary organizations like the Weathermen, the New Left does not have the type of organizational solidarity and commitment to enforce any given socialist strategy on its members. The New Left is more of a social movement, with members that come and go without much restriction, than a revolutionary organization parallel to Leninist parties.

In spite of the lack of commitment to any specific socialist strategy, it is possible to see a form of pluralistic or democratic socialism emerging among those associated with the New Left. Although the New Left has a commitment to equality, it also has another commitment to cultural and social diversity. The New Left (to some extent opposed to the Old Left) recognizes the legitimacy of various "factions" within the movement. Ethnic and national groups, women's liberation groups, groups based on age differences, as well as the white male group are all acceptable to the New Left. However, there is a potential tension between the goals of equality and diversity—that is, if the New Left is committed to equality, how can it handle the problem of unequal power and privileges distributed to each of these otherwise "legitimate" groups?

One of the ways that has been used to maintain this dual commitment is for the New Left to support programs that reallocate power and privileges to the groups that presently are low on some stratification system. For example, many New Left publications have sympathetic articles on women's liberation. And few white members of the New Left would oppose increased enrollments in colleges for minority students. As a result, we think that the conception of distributing power and privileges to various groups is becoming the dominant definition of equality in the New Left.[20]

If this interpretation of the New Left's view of equality is correct, then we are able to get a glimpse of the type of socialist commitment most likely to arise in the New Left. This would be a sort of "pluralistic socialism" in which various factions would legitimately be part of the movement to press for their own special values and interests. This is already taking place on many colleges and universities in the United States that have contingents of the New Left. For example, the Department of Sociology at U. C. Berkeley has numerous caucuses to press for various special interests in the department; the Black Caucus, Chicano Caucus, Asian Caucus, Women's Caucus, (white) Radical Caucus, to name some of the major sub-groups involved. And in recent years, the editorial staff of the *Berkeley Journal of Sociology* has been comprised of members of various caucuses; a perusal of the articles lately would indicate inclusion of articles of interest to various caucuses, written by members of the given sub-group (e.g.; women, blacks). Dependimg on the issue, these various sub-groups will often lend varying degrees of support to each other. This does not mean that there are no conflicts between the sub-groups; conflicts can arise, for example, when one group feels other groups have not given enough support to their measures. However, each of these groups in the department is fully legitimate in the eyes of the other groups, and periodically they work together in a common cause.

However if the "pluralist" part of "pluralist socialism" is fairly easy to document, the "socialism" part is not. At this point these groups—even the clearly "radical" elements among them—have not worked out an overall socialist position. It is possible that the decade of the 1970s will witness attempts to work out such a socialist position, among the many possibilities. (In fact, the New American Movement is clearly a recent example of an attempt to work out a position of "democratic socialism," which has many pluralist elements in it.)[21] But for many activists the socialist commitment seems to amount to a general commitment to the above-specified definition of equality by making changes of the system.

Anarchism

The second positive thrust of the student movement mentioned by various commentators is anarchism. Like the heavy emphasis on the individual in The Port Huron Statement of SDS, the influential work of Marcuse has a strongly libertarian and anarchist flavor to it. Commenting on German student activist Rudi Dutschke's essay, "On Anti-authoritarianism," Oglesby states that it is "more Marcusean than Marxist in many of its features"[22]—that is, Dutschke's analysis has a strong emphasis on criticizing the repressive aspects of corporate capitalism. Throughout this chapter we have seen repeated calls for liberation of oppressed people by student activists, as well as calls for their own liberation from bureaucratic constraints, power structures, and so forth. These demands are all aspects of various activists' antagonism to external controls over individuals, especially by such agencies as the state. This antagonism to external controls is central to an anarchist position.

Horowitz has developed a "typology of anarchist strategies and beliefs."[23] Among the types of anarchism he discusses are utilitarian anarchism, peasant anarchism, anarcho-syndicalism, collectivist anarchism, conspiratorial anarchism, communist anarchism, individualist anarchism, and pacifist anarchism. Although all forms of anarchism are antagonistic to external controls and desire a situation in which individuals are free from constraints, there are differences in the strategies to arrive at the common "good society." Some of the differences that Horowitz lists are as follows:

Should the first step include or exclude violence? Should the State be liquidated as a consequence of workers' organization from below, or must the first stage in organizing a system of mutual aid be in terms of first liquidating the State? Should anarchism strive for victory through numbers or through conspiratorial techniques?[24]

It could be said with justification that Horowitz is describing issues of "Old Left anarchism." Yet an empirical survey—which we do not pretend to be able to do here—might reveal that some activists fall into at least some of Horowitz' categories of anarchists. For example, such groups as the Weathermen and the Symbionese Liberation Army might fit into his categories. However instead of speculating on that point, let us turn to a genuinely New Left brand of anarchy: a type of anarchy that could be called "hedonistic anarchy," which is represented by such activists as Jerry Rubin and Abbie Hoffman.

Abbie Hoffman shares the New Left's antagonism to capitalism, racism, imperialism, and corporate liberalism.[25] However, what he is "for" is long hair, "doing his own thing," freedom to smoke dope and have a "good time" and not be serious, and freedom from corporations.[26] He is even against the political organizers of the "political" New Left because of their seriousness of purpose. But the anarchism of Abbie Hoffman, Jerry Rubin, and the "Yippies" does share with the political aspect of the New Left an opposition to the entire social system of the United States. In fact, Hoffman even announced his group had set up a "new nation" in the United States (this is the "Woodstock Nation")![27]

The Role of Political Consciousness

In this chapter we have examined various dimensions of radical political consciousness found among activists in the New Left. It is clear that the "negative" component of radical ideology is more strongly developed than the "positive" aspect. In other words, there are clearer positions among New Left activists against capitalism, imperialism, power structures, and racism, than there are clear positions favoring socialism and anarchism. However, the positive and negative aspects are both dimensions of radical political consciousness because they involve attempts to increase freedom and equality for submerged groups by making a change of some social system. The negative elements are seen by New Left activists to impede the achievement of freedom and equality for submerged groups. As a result actions are often mobilized against some concrete expression of one of these systems (e.g., protests are made against Vietnam as an instance of U.S. imperialism). The positive elements are seen by at least some activists as strategies to overcome the negative forces and therefore help obtain freedom and equality for submerged groups. But the prominence of the negative component of the concept means that this component will be the main focus for our empirical index of radical political consciousness in the chapters to follow.

Since we feel that radical political consciousness is an important type of determinant of participating in student activism, we should specify its exact causal status in our analysis. In presenting evidence about radical ideology among student activists, we are not arguing that radical political consciousness—or reformist political consciousness—is an absolute requirement for engagement in activism. Nor are we arguing that radical or reformist political consciousness is sufficient for engagement in activism. We are, however, arguing that political consciousness—radical or reformist—is a very important *contributing* condition of activism that, in Smelser's theory of collective behavior, systematically combines with other conditions, such as structural conduciveness and structural strain, to explain the participation in student activism.[28]

The idea that political consciousness is a contributing but not a necessary or sufficient condition of activism is somewhat different than many other positions on the matter. Probably due to the controversial nature of the topic, there is a tendency toward reductionism in the literature on student activism—that is, one tends to find a variety of "single-factor" explanations of activism. Furthermore, the single-factor often involves: (1) some statement of the central importance of the activists' ideology in determining activism or (2) a statement of the epiphenomenal nature of the activists' ideology. For example, Flacks tends to view radical political consciousness as both a necessary and sufficient condition of activism;[29] Schwab tends to view educational reform ideology as a necessary and sufficient condition of activism;[30] and Gintis tends to view the combination of radical and educational reform ideologies—what we call radical-reformist political consciousness—as a necessary and sufficient condition of activism.[31] In contrast to these approaches, Feuer does not view political consciousness as a primary determinant of activism. Instead of seeing political consciousness as a necessary, sufficient, or contributing condition of activism, Feuer relies on a theory that emphasizes family conflicts as the main determinant of student activism.[32]

When we argue that political consciousness is an important contributing condition of activism, we are thus rejecting any type of reductionist position on activism. Although political consciousness contributes to the engagement in activism, it is not an all-determining condition of activism. For example, the percentage difference for the relationship between a student's radical political consciousness and student activism is e = 29 percent, with a Chi-Square of .001. This is a moderately strong two-variable relationship, but it is not an extremely strong relationship. On the other hand, approaches to activism that underemphasize the role of political consciousness have as many limitations as approaches that overemphasize political consciousness. Thus, when the three major types of political consciousness used in this study are combined, we find that 66 percent of those politically conscious are activists.

Hence, we can conclude that a middle-range social-psychological approach to student activism that emphasizes political consciousness is *both* a useful approach and a limited approach. It is useful by pointing to the positive role of political consciousness in determining activism, but it is limited because other variables must be taken into account for a fuller explanation of activism. Thus, it is necessary to *combine* a middle-range social-psychological approach with a structural and historical approach to obtain the fuller explanation of student activism. To do this, in the last chapter we employ Smelser's theory of collective behavior, which shows how generalized beliefs such as political consciousness systematically combine with other conditions such as precipitating factors, and the weakening of social control to broadly explain collective behavior like student activism.

In sum, we feel that there are important links between radical ideology of parents, radical ideology of the student, and student activism, given the historical situation of the Sixties. But there are other approaches to student activism that stress quite different variables such as educational structure, the rise of a new working class of educated laborers, social alienation, and cultural alienation. In the empirical chapters that follow the quantitative data indicate the strengths and weaknesses of the various approaches to activism. In the process, we hope to show the general utility of our own approach to activism, spelled out in the last two chapters, and the relative weakness of the other approaches.

Notes

1. Although some would question our using the terms political consciousness and political ideology synonymously, there is a literature that supports this usage. For example, Geertz notes that the concept of ideology is frequently used to mean "sociopolitical ideas." Similarly, Apter states that " 'Ideology' is a generic term applied to general ideas in specific

situations of conduct: for example, not any ideals, only political ones.'' See Clifford Geertz, ''Ideology as a Cultural System,'' in David E. Apter, ed., *Ideology and Discontent* (New York: The Free Press, 1964), p. 52; and David E. Apter, ''Introduction: Ideology and Discontent,'' in Apter, ibid., p. 17.

2. The concept of ''change *in* the social system'' refers to reformist political consciousness, which will be discussed in later chapters. Also a desire to make changes *in* the system and a change *of* the system is called by us radical-reformist political consciousness, which is also discussed later.

3. See, for example, Richard C. Edwards, Michael Reich, and Thomas E. Weisskopf, eds., *The Capitalist System* (Englewood Cliffs, N.J.: Prentice-Hall, 1972). Also see various recent editions of *The Insurgent Sociologist* for Marxist, anti-capitalist analyses of various phenomena. Similarly, see the various papers given at The Second Annual Socialist Sociology Conference, The San Jose YMCA Camp, Camp Cambell, Boulder Creek, California, May 23 to 27, 1974.

4. Clark Kerr, *The Uses of the University* (Cambridge, Mass.: Harvard University Press, 1964).

5. For books stressing some version of the imperialist theory of U.S. involvement in Vietnam, see David Horowitz, *The Free World Colossus: A Critique of American Foreign Policy in the Cold War* (London: MacGibbon & Kee, 1965), pp. 141-162; David Horowitz, *Empire and Revolution: A Radical Interpretation of Contemporary History* (New York: Random House, 1969), pp. 193-258; Gabriel Kolko, *The Roots of American Foreign Policy* (Boston: Beacon Press, 1969), pp. 88-132; Paul A. Baran and Paul M. Sweezy, *Monopoly Capital* (New York: Monthly Review Press, 1966), pp. 178-217, 364-367; Harry Magdoff, *The Age of Imperialism* (New York: Monthly Review Press, 1969); and, less directly, Franz Schurmann, Peter Dale Scott, and Reginald Zelnik, *The Politics of Escalation in Vietnam* (Boston: Beacon Press, 1966).

6. Stokely Carmichael and Charles V. Hamilton, *Black Power: The Politics of Liberation in America* (New York: Vintage Books, A Division of Random House, 1967), p. 4.

7. Ibid., pp. 41-42.

8. Ibid., pp. 44-45; and Nathan Glazer and Daniel Patrick Moynihan, *Beyond the Melting Pot* (Cambridge, Mass.: The M.I.T. Press, 1963), ''Preface,'' ''Introduction,'' and ''Beyond the Melting Pot,'' pp. v-vi, 1-23, 288-315.

9. C. Wright Mills, *The Power Elite* (New York: Oxford University Press, A Galaxy Book, 1956, 1959).

10. ''The Port Huron Statement'' of SDS presented at Port Huron, Michigan in 1962, cited in Marvin B. Scott and Stanford M. Lyman, *The*

Revolt of the Students (Columbus, Ohio: Charles E. Merrill Publishing Co., 1970), p. 43.

11. See "The Port Huron Statement" of SDS in Scott and Lyman, ibid., pp. 45-46.

12. Scott and Lyman, ibid., pp. 40-41.

13. Alphonso Pinkney, *The Committed: White Activists in the Civil Rights Movement* (New Haven: College and University Press, 1968), p. 47.

14. See James L. Wood, "The Role of Radical Political Consciousness in Student Political Activism: A Preliminary Analysis," Contributed Paper presented at the 66th Annual Meeting of the American Sociological Association, Denver, Colorado, 1971.

15. See Richard Flacks, "The Liberated Generation: An Exploration of the Roots of Student Protest," *The Journal of Social Issues* 23 (July 1967): 52-75; Glen Lyonns, "The Police Car Demonstration: A Survey of Participants," in Seymour Martin Lipset and Sheldon S. Wolin, eds., *The Berkeley Student Revolt* (Garden City, N.Y.: Anchor Books, 1965), pp. 519-530; Paul B. Miller, "Revolutionists Among the Chicago Demonstrators," *American Journal of Psychiatry* 127, No. 6 (December, 1970): 752-58; and John L. Horn and Paul D. Knott, "Activist Youth of the 1960's: Summary and Prognosis," *Science* 171 (March 12, 1971): pp. 977-85, for empirical evidence of a socialist commitment among at least some members of the New Left.

16. Miller, op. cit., pp. 752-54.

17. Flacks, op. cit., pp. 66-68.

18. Carl Oglesby, "Introduction: The Idea of The New Left," in Carl Oglesby, ed., *The New Left Reader* (New York: Grove Press, 1969), p. 17.

19. The first meeting to discuss developing a socialist sociology was held in Denver, Colorado, at the 1971 ASA meeting. See the Preliminary Program of the Annual Meeting of the American Sociological Association, Denver, Colorado, August 30 to September 2, 1971, Session 53, p. 36. The lead paper of this session was published in *The Insurgent Sociologist*. See Richard Flacks, "Towards a Socialist Sociology: Some Proposals for Work in the Coming Period," *The Insurgent Sociologist,* Vol. II, No. 2 (January-February 1972): 12-27. Subsequent meetings to discuss socialist sociology have been held at the 1972 meeting of the Pacific Sociological Association in Portland, Oregon, and at the 1972 meeting of the American Sociological Association in New Orleans, Louisiana.

20. There are, of course, various other definitions of equality than redistributing power and privileges to various groups. For example, two other definitions of equality would be equality of opportunity, and equality before the law. The concept of equality of opportunity usually implies *acceptance* of unequal distribution of power and privileges, but it rejects

such factors as group membership as legitimate influences in the competition for scarce resources. Equality before the law does not really address the issue of distribution of resources.

21. For a discussion of the New American Movement, see Theirrie Cook and Michael P. Lerner, "The New American Movement," *Social Policy* 3 (July-August 1972): 27-31, 54-56. Lerner has also written a book on the topic: *The New Socialist Revolution* (New York: Delacorte Press, 1973).

22. See Carl Oglesby commenting on Rudi Dutschke, "On Anti-authoritarianism," in Oglesby, op. cit., p. 243.

23. Irving L. Horowitz, "Introduction" to *The Anarchists,* edited by Irving L. Horowitz (New York: Dell Publishing Co., A Laurel Original, 1964), pp. 28-55.

24. Horowitz, ibid., p. 29.

25. Abbie Hoffman, *Woodstock Nation* (New York: Random House, 1969), p. 8.

26. Ibid.

27. Ibid., pp. 4-8.

28. See Neil J. Smelser, *Theory of Collective Behavior* (New York: The Free Press of Glencoe, 1963); and Neil J. Smelser, "Social and Psychological Dimensions of Collective Behavior," in his *Essays in Sociological Explanation* (Englewood Cliffs, N.J.: Prentice-Hall, 1968), Chapter Five, pp. 92-121.

29. Flacks, "The Liberated Generation," op. cit.

30. Joseph J. Schwab, *College Curriculum and Student Protest* (Chicago: The University of Chicago Press, 1969).

31. Herbert Gintis, "The New Working Class and Revolutionary Youth," *Continuum* 8 (Spring-Summer 1970): 151-74.

32. Lewis S. Feuer, *The Conflict of Generations* (New York: Basic Books, 1969).

4 Methodological Considerations

This chapter focuses on the methodological assumptions and strategies involved in testing the specific theories of student activism. These strategies will be employed throughout the rest of the book, although specific chapters will additionally discuss other methodological issues as is necessary.

As stated in Chapter 1, student political activism is generally defined as the engagement by students in non-institutionalized political activities, such as illegal demonstrations against the Vietnam War and sit-ins. The focus of this definition is on concrete political *actions* by students, as distinct from their political *ideas*. It is important to distinguish ideas from actions because much of the analysis in this study concerns the relationship between ideas and actions. Thus, to avoid tautological reasoning it is necessary to separate mental processes (such as ideas) from concrete behavior (such as activism) in order to study their interrelationship.

In reference to the empirical data on Berkeley activism, the operational definition of student political activism is based on the students' responses to the portion of the 1968 questionnaire asking whether or not they had taken part in the following political activities:

1. Various aspects of the Free Speech Movement in 1964-65.
2. The Student Strike in December 1966, which occurred after the conflict centering on the ROTC recruiting table that was set up in the Student Union on the Berkeley campus.
3. The Oakland Induction Center demonstration in the Fall of 1967.

Any student who took part in one of these events is considered an activist in this study. The reason students were not required to take part in two or even three of the activities to be considered activists is due to the fact many students were not on campus for each event. Thus, even though a given student might have wanted to participate in, say, the Free Speech Movement, his absence from campus during that time period prevented his activity. However, analysis of the data indicates that the variables associated with engagement in only one instance of activism are similarly associated with engagement in two or three instances of activism. Actually, the association between variables increases somewhat as a student participated in more instances of activism. But the direction of the association of variables is similar whether a student participated in one, two, or three instances of activism. Appendix B discusses further technicalities of the definition of student political activism.

Each of the three items in the operational definition of activism was a concrete, observable political event of a "non-institutionalized" nature. Each involved some aspects of political confrontation outside the framework of presently legitimate institutional politics. For example, the protests at the Induction Center included a sit-in that attempted to prevent army inductees from entering the Induction Center, which brought about the arrest and imprisonment of various students who did not "follow the rules" to achieve political change. (Instead of voting in peace candidates, for example, the students engaged in illegal activities in their efforts to help end the war.) The arrest of 800 demonstrators in Sproul Hall is another dramatic example of the illegitimacy of non-institutionalized activity. And finally, the idea of a student strike, as opposed to a workers' strike, is not yet institutionalized and is also considered by many as illegitimate. Although other studies operationally define student activism with other concrete events, most studies usually refer to some instance of non-institutionalized political activity of students.

Student political activism is the main dependent variable used in this study. Only on special occasions will student activism be treated as an independent variable. Although most theorists interpret their data as if activism were the dependent variable, or the phenomenon to be explained, it is not uncommon to see tables set up *as if* activism were the independent variable, or the phenomenon which explains something else. For example, in "The Liberated Generation," Flacks sets up his own tables incorrectly in view of his theory of activism: activism versus non-activism is presented by Flacks as though the variable were the independent variable, although he interprets his results as though activism versus non-activism were the dependent variable.[1] In our tables activism will be the dependent variable unless otherwise stated. Finally, in most of our tables, only data on student activists are reported, although the figures are computed from the entire random sample of activists and non-activists ($N = 492$).

We use percentage difference (e) as our principal measure of statistical association in the various tables. However, when necessary from a methodological standpoint, other measures of association, such as Somers' dyx, are used. In addition to these measures of association, we report Chi-Square tests of statistical significance (χ^2) that are significant at the .10 level or better; Chi-Squares that do not reach the .10 level will be designated as Not Significant (N.S.).

The primary method used to examine the theories of activism is the "elaboration schema" originated by Paul Lazarsfeld, codified by Herbert Hyman, and developed and extended by Charles Y. Glock, Morris Rosenberg, Travis Hirschi and Hanan C. Selvin, and others.[2] The logic of this system is to first examine two-variable relationships and then introduce third (or more) variables to "test" the original two-variable relationship. Since many of the conclusions in the literature on activism are based on two-variable relationships, we hope that the introduction of various third variables to test the original two-variable relationships is a methodological, as well as substantive, improvement on much of the prior literature.

The use of the elaboration schema depends on clear statements of the independent, intervening, and dependent variables in a given model. We spell out the theories of activism in terms of the stated or implied variables in order to effectively use the elaboration schema to help test the theories. The basic components of the elaboration schema are (1) explanation, (2) interpretation, (3) replication, and (4) specification. Each of these are possible statistical outcomes when a third variable is introduced to "test" the original two-variable relationship. Each of these four components of the elaboration schema are defined in the following paragraphs.

As classically defined, *explanation* refers to the situation where the introduction of a third variable "explains away" the original two-variable relationship. The original two-variable relationship existed statistically only because both variables were related to a third variable. Thus the original relationship is felt to be a spurious (i.e., invalid) relationship. Statistically, the original relationship is reduced in all "partial tables" when the third variable is introduced; in the extreme case, the original relationship entirely disappears in all the partial tables. One final aspect of the explanation component of the elaboration schema: the third variable must precede in time both the original independent and dependent variables. If the third variable can explain away the original relationship, the third variable must come before either variable whose value depends upon this third variable.

The next form of elaboration is *interpretation*. Here the third variable is seen as intervening between the independent and dependent variables. It is the link between the independent variable and the dependent variable, not a variable prior in time that could explain away the original relationship. However, interpretation does have an important similarity with explanation. We expect the original statistical relationship to be reduced in all partial tables. But the meaning of this statistical reduction of the original relationship is quite different for interpretation than for explanation. For interpretation, the original two-variable relationship is seen as valid; the procedure is aimed at uncovering the mechanism that links the independent and dependent variables. The third variable intervenes between the independent variable and the dependent variable both logically and temporally.

The third form of elaboration is *replication*. This means that the original relationship remains virtually the same in all partial tables. If the investigator expected a reduction in the partial tables for a presumed interpretation of the original relationship and he got a statistical result of replication, he would have to reject his interpretation. However, replication can also provide evidence for the validity of an original relationship. For example, it is possible for a relationship to be replicated when a third variable was felt capable of explaining away the original relationship. The replication of the original relationship in all partial tables provides evidence of its validity and evidence against its spurious quality.

The final major form of elaboration discussed by Hyman is *specification*. Specification states conditions under which the original relationship becomes more or less pronounced when a third variable is introduced. Specification does not rely as much on the importance of time order of the variables as does explanation and interpretation. For example, if a relationship is seen between social class and voting behavior, it is possible to ask if this relationship is more pronounced for men than women. Again, a third variable—this time sex of the respondent—is introduced to specify the original relationship.

We introduce key "test variables" to see whether the various two-variable relationships suggested by the theories of activism can be replicated, interpreted, explained away, or specified. Flacks and many other empirical investigators of student activism only focus on two-variable relationships.[3] As a result, Flacks and these other investigators usually wind up with a "list" of characteristics of activists and non-activists. The focus on two-variable relationships makes it easy to compare activists and non-activists in a descriptive fashion.[4] But when one decides to analytically test theories of activism, it is necessary to go beyond the elementary two-variable relationship and use such techniques as introducing various third test variables into the original two-variable relationship. However, when one turns to analysis of this sort, student activism becomes the dependent variable because it is the phenomenon to be explained; a list of characteristics of activists and non-activists is no longer the goal of the research.[5]

A few comments should be made here about what we mean by "testing" theories of activism. Sellitz et al. have stated three conditions necessary to meet to infer causal relationships between two variables.[6] The three conditions are (1) concomitant variation of the variables, (2) time order of the variables wherein the presumed "cause" precedes in time the presumed "effect," and (3) the elimination of other possible causal factors than the presumed cause. Since it is never possible to eliminate all other possible causes of the dependent variable, we can only say we infer causality, not positively prove causality. In addition, in our data at least, many of the two-variable relationships are not clearly of one time order. This is especially the case when the relationship is between attitudes and behavior; our own position is that attitudes and behavior are interdependent, not only of one time order. Thus, we often make statements about relation-ships and associations betwen variables instead of one-way causal state-ments. However, in order for any theory of activism to receive substantia-tion in our data, the variables must be associated empirically to the extent and in the direction predicted by the theory. If the variables are not associated to the proper extent or in the predicted direction, then there is evidence against the theory; if the variables are associated to the proper extent and in the predicted direction, then there is evidence—although not "ultimate proof," of course—for the validity of the theory.

Our data are most useful in examining the empirical associations be-tween the variables and in helping to eliminate other possible causes of the dependent variable. They are least useful in establishing time order of the variables. However, in many relationships we examine, the time order of the variables is reasonably clear (e.g., the social class background of the activists clearly precedes their engagement in activism). Furthermore, the literature on causal inferences usually discusses a fourth condition that helps provide evidence on causality, although it is not felt to be as "neces-sary" for causal inferences as the first three conditions discussed. This fourth condition is the statement of intervening mechanisms that link the independent and dependent variables.[7] Our data are able to directly ad-dress many of the theories of activism that take a stand on the mechanisms that link the independent and dependent variables. Thus, these data are able to help test theories of activism by providing evidence on many of the conditions of causal inference.

Before proceeding to the data analysis, a few more points about the data should be mentioned. Common to almost all surveys (but not common to all published discussions of surveys), our survey must handle the problem of "missing data." That is, not every item was answered by every respon-dent; hence, the problem of missing data. This problem is magnified by the fact that there are three separate but interrelated instruments—one for the students and two for their parents. The response rate for parents was approximately 60 percent of the student sample, as Appendix A indicates. Thus, when we examine relationships between parents and students, we have missing data for approximately 40 percent of the parents and students. This might suggest many biases for parents who returned the mailed ques-tionnaire and Q-Sort versus those who did not. Fortunately, this was not the case. We compared student responses on 54 items for students whose parents responded versus students whose parents did not respond to Somers' parental questionnaire (similar conclusions would be reached for Block's parental Q-Sort). On only 10 out of the 54 items was there a percentage difference of as much as 10 percent between students whose parents responded versus students whose parents did not respond. Actu-ally the highest recorded percentage difference was only 12 percent. The only slight biases seemed to be that parents who were less-educated, blue-collar in occupation, and Asian in ethnic background, tended to be less likely than others to respond. But even in these cases the differences were not large. Hence the parental instruments contain missing data, but the missing data are generally unbiased.

There is another aspect of missing data of which the reader should be aware when he interprets the various tables. Occasionally, the same two-variable relationship is presented more than one time, as in Tables 5-3 and 5-5, which show the relationship between parents' liberal ideology and student activism. It would not be unreasonable to think the tables are redundant; however, a different third variable is introduced into the original relationship. Thus, in Table 5-4 we introduce student's radical political consciousness as the third variable, whereas in Table 5-6 we introduce student's liberal ideology as the third variable. If everyone had answered the items related to both third variables, it would not be necessary to present the same original relationship twice. However, there were a few people who answered the items for student's radical political consciousness, but not for student's liberal ideology, and vice versa. As a result, we have the problem of missing data. The missing data is reflected in slightly different percentages from one table to the next and/or slightly different absolute numbers from one table to the next. For example, the original relationship between mother's liberal ideology and student activism in Table 5-3 is e = 24 percent, whereas it is e = 23 percent in Table 5-5. In addition, the absolute number of cases for fathers who are high on liberal ideology in Table 5-3 is 23, whereas it is 22 in Table 5-5. The computer program used, Table-Y from the Survey Research Center at U. C. Berkeley, repeated the original two-variable relationship for each of the relationships where we introduced a third variable. Thus, it was possible to report the exact figures for each set of relationships as we have done. This aspect of missing data does not occur often, but it could be confusing to the reader when he sees slightly different statistics presented for the same relationship.

Finally, many of the concepts used in this analysis are measured by indices formed by items listed in Appendix C. The various Gamma scores showing the association between the items of the indices are included in Appendix C.

Notes

1. Richard Flacks, "The Liberated Generation: An Exploration of the Roots of Student Protest," *The Journal of Social Issues* 23 (July 1967: 52-75.

2. The original statement of the elaboration schema was by Paul Lazarsfeld at the Cleveland meeting of the American Sociological Society in 1946. It was published for the first time as Patricia L. Kendall and Paul F. Lazarsfeld, "Problems of Survey Analysis," in Robert K. Merton and Paul F. Lazarsfeld, eds., *Continuities in Social Research: Studies in the Scope and Method of "The American Soldier"* (Glencoe, Ill.: The Free Press, 1950), pp. 133-96. This methodology was codified in Herbert Hyman's *Survey Design and Analysis* copyright 1955 by The Free Press, Chapters VI and VII, pp. 242-329. The elaboration schema has been developed and extended by Morris Rosenberg, *The Logic of Survey Analysis* (New York: Basic Books, 1968); Charles Y. Glock, ed., *Survey Research in the Social Sciences* (New York: Russell Sage Foundation, 1967); Travis Hirschi and Hanan C. Selvin, *Delinquency Research: An Appraisal of Analytic Methods* (New York: The Free Press, 1967), among others.

3. Recently more sophisticated statistical techniques have been used in the analysis of activism. See the description of the methodological techniques in the studies summarized in Kenneth Keniston, *Radicals and Militants: An Annotated Bibliography of Empirical Research on Campus Unrest* (Lexington, Mass.: Lexington Books, D.C. Heath, 1973). Also see the discussion in note 4 of this chapter.

4. Many empirical discussions of student activism present a "list" of items that characterizes activists, or activists versus non-activists. Thus two-variable analysis has been quite typical. Besides Flacks' "The Liberated Generation," op. cit., see: David Westby and Richard Braungart, "Activists and the History of the Future," in Julian Foster and Durward Long, eds., *Protest!: Student Activism in America* (New York: William Morrow & Co., 1970), pp. 158-83; Riley Dunlap, "Radical and Conservative Student Activists: A Comparison of Family Backgrounds," *Pacific Sociological Review* 13 (Summer 1970): 171-81; and Paul R. Miller, "Social Activists and Social Change: The Chicago Demonstrators," *American Journal of Psychiatry* 126, No. 12 (June 1970): 94-101. An exception is the dissertation of Milton Mankoff. Mankoff introduces many third variables to test his original two-variable relationships. See Milton L. Mankoff, "The Political Socialization of Radicals and Militants in the Wisconsin Student Movement During the 1960's," unpublished Ph.D. dissertation, Department of Sociology, University of Wisconsin, 1969. However, even Mankoff does not usually have a "theoretical" reason for introducing his third variables; he just introduces them without specifying what he hopes to prove. We hope to have more theoretical justification for introducing our series of third variables to test for the initial relationship (e.g., between father's radical consciousness and student activism). Finally, Richard G. Braungart has applied the methodology of path analysis to the study of student activism, which clearly is one of the most sophisticated attempts to

date to use multivariate techniques in the understanding of activism. See his "Family Status, Socialization, and Student Politics: A Multivariate Analysis," *American Journal of Sociology* 77 (July 1971): 108-130. A most interesting comparison would be between Braungart's use of path analysis in the study of activism and the elaboration schema methodology of introducing key "test variables." Both methods, in their separate ways, transcend the methodology of two-variable analysis that has tended to characterize the study of activism.

5. We have run some of the tables in our data with student activism both as the dependent variable and as the independent variable to see whether the percentage differences in two-variable relationships were very different. Fortunately the percentage differences were quite similar when, for example, student activism was run against political consciousness and when political consciousness was run against student activism.

6. Claire Selltiz, Marie Jahoda, Morton Deutsch, and Stuart W. Cook, *Research Methods in Social Relations,* Revised One-Volume Edition (New York: Holt, Rinehart and Winston, 1951, 1959), pp. 83-88.

7. Ibid., pp. 427-9.

5

The Family, Political Ideology, and Student Activism

Introduction

The family has been shown to be implicated in student activism in many studies. Theorists have probably chosen the family as a central determinant of activism as often as the structure of the modern multiversity. However, there are many different and contradictory ways that the family has been seen as a source of student activism. Even though two or more theorists might agree that the family is important in understanding participation in student protests, they might strongly disagree on *how* the family contributes to activism. Is it due to the socialization to a radical or liberal set of political values? Or is it because activists are rebelling against their parents? Similarly, do the parents teach their children a set of unconventional—but unpolitical—cultural values that get translated into activism? Or does activism arise in relation to overly permissive childrearing practices? Finally, is activism the result of a distinctive—and often favored—social-economic background? In the next few chapters, we empirically examine these contrasting ways that the family has been seen to influence student activism.

The greatest empirical support is for two approaches that have previously been seen as antagonistic. Our data indicate support for the approach focusing on the radical socialization of activists *and* the approach focusing on the conflict of generations. The other family approaches either receive less support in the data or no support at all. These findings do provide evidence for our argument that many activists act out radical political values derived from their parents' radical political or culturally unconventional values; but they also come into conflict with their parents because the activists feel the parents have not lived up to their own political or cultural values.

Political Background of Activists

Various commentators such as Flacks, Lipset, and Keniston have argued that student activists were socialized in politically liberal or radical families. The students are said to adhere to the left-wing political views of their parents, and in the face of political crises, these views get translated into student activism on university and college campuses. This chapter

47

empirically examines this approach to student activism. Although the approach has some important limitations, it also amounts to one of the stronger middle-range theories of activism in the literature.

This "left-wing socialization" approach to activism is often supported by empirical studies showing that activists tend to come from the same "left" side of the political spectrum as their parents. This approach usually deals with two types of left-wing political ideologies: (1) radical political consciousness and (2) reformist political consciousness. As defined earlier, radical political consciousness refers to those who want to obtain greater freedom and equality for submerged groups through making a change *of* the social system. Reformist political consciousness refers to those who want to obtain greater freedom and equality for submerged groups through making changes *in* the social system.

One of the most cited studies in support of the left-wing socialization hypothesis is Richard Flacks' "The Liberated Generation."[1] Flacks contrasts activists with non-activists on their views about political issues that were current in 1965-66 (his article was published in 1967). Some of these issues were U.S. bombings of North Vietnam, student participation in protest demonstrations, full socialization of industry, congressional investigations of "un-American activities," attitudes toward presidential candidates Lyndon Johnson and Barry Goldwater, socialization of the medical profession, civil disobedience in civil rights protests, and American troops sent to the Dominican Republic.[2] His data show that on each item the activists are more "radical" or "liberal" than the non-activists. Similarly, his data show that the families of activists are more radical or liberal than the families of non-activists. Specifically, he found that activists tend to come from liberal or radical families whereas non-activists tend to come from more conservative or "moderate" families.[3] He says that "activists and their fathers tend to be at least 'liberal,'" and in comparison

. . . the non-activist sample is only slightly less conservative and Republican than their fathers . . . and both non-activists and their fathers are typically "moderate" in their politics.[4]

Although Flacks shows activists and their parents come from the same general "side" of the political spectrum (i.e., the "left" side rather than the "right" side), he also notes that "Activists are more 'radical' than their parents."[5] As a result of these findings, Flacks must come to a dual set of conclusions. On one hand he must admit a somewhat greater statistical correspondence on his questionnaire items between parents and children of non-activists than between parents and children of activists.[6] But he also argues cogently that activists do come from "left-wing" families more so than non-activists. And from this fact he concludes that

. . . most students who are involved in the movement (at least those one finds in a city like Chicago) are involved in neither "conversion" from nor "rebellion" against the political perspectives of their fathers.[7]

Instead, he argues that "A more supportable view suggests that the great majority of these students are attempting to fulfill and renew the political traditions of their families."[8] Thus, he feels his study supports the idea of value continuity between the generations for politically active students —they are fulfilling their parents' values, not revolting against them.

There have been many other studies indicating that left-wing activists were socialized in politically radical or liberal families. Along with Flacks' study, Keniston's work on activism has been frequently cited in this connection.[9] Similar to Flacks, Keniston sees activists acting out the leftist political values of their parents. Although he also sees some ambivalences in the relationship between activists and their parents, Keniston concludes that "what is most impressive is the solidarity of older and younger generations."[10]

In a useful review of the literature, Lipset cites various studies that conclude left activists come from leftist backgrounds.[11] For example, he cites the Harris Survey of Students in 1970 with regard to the widespread protests over Cambodia. In this survey, 80 percent of the students whose mother's ideology was "Far Left" participated in the protests. Also 69 percent of the students whose mother's ideology was "Liberal" participated in the protests. In contrast, only half of the students whose mother's ideology was "Conservative" or "Far Right" participated in the Cambodian protests (parenthetically, we should note that in almost no other student protest of the past decade were there as many activists of conservative background as in the Cambodian protests, which thus testifies to the truly widespread nature of that particular national protest).[12] Similarly, Lipset cites Cowdry and Keniston who feel that the Yale students "most likely to hold radical beliefs *and* act on them" are those whose fathers have similar views.[13] And again Keniston is cited: ". . . *if* the parents are themselves politically liberal and politically active, then the chances of the child's being an activist are greatly increased."[14] In sum, Lipset concludes that "in the United States . . . leftist students are largely the children of leftist or liberal parents."[15]

Recently two important book-length bibliographies on student activism have been published. These bibliographies—organized by Altbach and Kelly, and by Keniston—contain various studies that also support the left-wing socialization hypothesis.[16] For example, the following studies are discussed as supporting this hypothesis: Braungart, Aron, Astin, Westby and Braungart, Somers, and Allerbeck.[17] Although a few studies do not lend as much support to the hypothesis,[18] the overall tendency in the literature suggests that left activists come from left-wing political backgrounds.

Although these studies amount to evidence for activists coming from radical *or* liberal left-wing families, we feel that a distinction should be made between radical and liberal families. The literature on activism usually blurs these two different types of political viewpoints as "leftist" viewpoints. We have seen, for example, that Keniston concludes that activists come from both radical backgrounds and from liberal backgrounds.[19] Similarly, Lipset often uses the phrase "liberal-to-left" to describe the political background of activists.[20] In trying to reject the conflict of generations approach to activism, Flacks argues that activists come from the same left side of the political spectrum as their parents—that is, the activists' parents were shown to be radical or liberal in political orientation.[21] To be sure, many of these theorists state that activists are more radical in their views than their parents.[22] But there is a tendency, nevertheless, to either blur radical and liberal parental views, or to argue they have an identical impact on activists. We show that it is essential to *distinguish* these political orientations in trying to see how family ideology does contribute to activism.

Frequently, two-variable analysis of data is used to support the thesis that activists come from radical or liberal families.[23] Our use of the more sophisticated elaboration schema methodology indicates that *radical* ideology of the parents (and the activists themselves) is clearly more associated with activism than liberal ideology of the parents or students. Those who use two-variable (or even more complex) analysis frequently do not even look for a distinction between the impact of radical and liberal parents, which we feel is essential.

Radical Socialization

In order to examine the impact of either radical or liberal parental ideology on activism, it is necessary to have clear statements of the relevant independent, dependent, and intervening variables. To test the radical socialization approach to activism, we would say that radical political consciousness of the parents is the independent variable, student activism is the dependent variable, and radical political consciousness of the student is the intervening variable. Put diagramatically the argument looks like this:

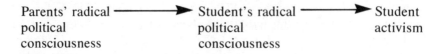

Parents' radical political consciousness ⟶ Student's radical political consciousness ⟶ Student activism

There should be an initial relationship between parents' radical political consciousness and student activism (i.e., an initial relationship between the independent and dependent variables). In this model, student's radical political consciousness is seen as the intervening link between the independent and dependent variables. Hence a finding of "interpretation" in the terminology of the elaboration schema would be expected. When we hold constant student's radical political consciousness as the intervening third variable, the original relationship should be reduced in all partial tables for the anticipated interpretation actually to occur. This in fact happens in our data when either father or mother is considered, as Tables 5-1 and 5-2 indicate. The original relationship between father's radical political consciousness and student activism is $e = 19$ percent. When the student's radical political consciousness is introduced as the intervening variable, the original relationship of $e = 19$ percent drops to 9 percent in one partial table and to 8 percent in the other partial table. The original relationship between mother's radical political consciousness and student activism is $e = 15$ percent. When student's radical political consciousness is introduced as the third variable, the original relationship of $e = 15$ percent drops to 4 percent in one partial table and to 8 percent in the other partial table. Following Hyman, we would take these findings as evidence supporting the notion that many activists are socialized to a radical perspective by their radically conscious parents. When the third variable—here, student's radical political consciousness—was held constant, the original relationship between parental radical political consciousness and student activism was reduced in all partial tables. Therefore, we do see evidence for links between radical ideology of parents, radical ideology of students, and student activism. Hence many activists can be seen as acting out their parents' radical political values.

Liberal Socialization

It is possible that radical consciousness of activists can come from socialization by liberal parents as well as radical parents. Many of the theorists who lump liberal and radical parents together under the heading of "leftist" parents expect radical student views to emerge from either radical or liberal families. Then the student is seen to translate these radical views into student activism. However, our data do not lend much support to the position that radical consciousness emerges from liberal families and later leads to activism. Restating this argument in a form amenable for testing by the elaboration schema, we would expect:

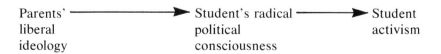

Parents' ⟶ Student's radical ⟶ Student
liberal   political   activism
ideology   consciousness

Table 5-1
Parents' Radical Political Consciousness and Student Activism

	Parent		
	Father		
Student Activism	Radical Consciousness		
	High	Low	
Active	(11)	(44)	e = 19%
	52%	33%	χ^2 = .10
Total	(21)	(134)	
	100%	100%	
	Mother		
Student Activism	Radical Consciousness		
	High	Low	
Active	(23)	(41)	e = 15%
	47%	32%	χ^2 = .10
Total	(49)	(130)	
	100%	100%	

The original relationship in our data is positive between both father's and mother's liberal ideology and student activism, as would be predicted. But when the supposed linking variable of radical political consciousness of the student is introduced, the expected interpretation does not occur for fathers and occurs only slightly for mothers. In fact, the finding of interpretation for mothers occurs only because there is "interpretation by specification," which will be discussed later in relation to parental humanitarianism and activism. The classic way to establish interpretation is for the original relationship between liberal parental ideology and student activism to become significantly reduced in all partial tables. However, interpretation can also be established by the original relationship significantly increasing under a given predicted condition such as high radical consciousness of the student. As Tables 5-3 and 5-4 show, the original relationship of e = 16 percent for fathers only decreases in one partial table and slightly increases in the other partial table. For mothers, there is a more pronounced increase of the original relationship of e = 24 percent under the condition of high radical consciousness of the student. Thus, the original relationship does not drop in both partial tables for mothers, but there is some "interpretation by specification" because of the increase of the original relation.

Table 5-2

Parents' Radical Political Consciousness and Student Activism, with Student's Radical Political Consciousness Controlled

Student's Radical Consciousness

	High			Low		
Student Activism	Father's Rad. Cons.			Father's Rad. Cons.		
	High	Low		High	Low	
Active	(9) 64%	(27) 56%	e = 8% χ² = N.S.	(2) 29%	(17) 20%	e = 9% χ² = N.S.
Total	(14) 100%	(48) 100%		(7) 100%	(86) 100%	

Student's Radical Consciousness

	High			Low		
Student Activism	Mother's Rad. Cons.			Mother's Rad. Cons.		
	High	Low		High	Low	
Active	(19) 59%	(24) 51%	e = 8% χ² = N.S.	(4) 24%	(17) 20%	e = 4% χ² = N.S.
Total	(32) 100%	(47) 100%		(17) 100%	(83) 100%	

In sum, there is a two-variable relation between liberal parental ideology and student activism, but radical consciousness of the student is not a strong linking mechanism. The original relationship may be perfectly valid, but some other linking mechanism would have to be operative. It is obvious that the other linking mechanism between parents' liberal ideology and student activism could be the student's liberal (as distinguished from radical) ideology.

There are weak links between father's liberal ideology, student's liberal ideology, and student activism, as Tables 5-5 and 5-6 indicate; however, no such links exist for mothers. For fathers, the original relationship of e = 16 percent drops to 11 percent in one partial table and to 9 percent in the other partial table. For mothers, there is a drop in the original relationship of e = 23 percent in only one partial table, and almost no change in the other partial table.

Due to the theoretical importance of the links between liberal parental

Table 5-3
Parents' Liberal Ideology and Student Activism

Student Activism	Parent		
	Father		
	Liberal Ideology		
	High	Low	
Active	(23) 46%	(31) 30%	e = 16% χ^2 = .10
Total	(50) 100%	(103) 100%	
Student Activism	Mother		
	Liberal Ideology		
	High	Low	
Active	(29) 51%	(33) 27%	e = 24% χ^2 = .01
Total	(57) 100%	(121) 100%	

ideology, liberal student ideology, and student activism, other tables were run to see whether stronger positive relations might turn up. However, the following relations do not receive empirical substantiation in our data: (1) civil rights reformist views of the parents, civil rights reformist views of the student, and student activism or (2) educational reform views of the parents, educational reform views of the student, and student activism (see Table 5-7). Using a somewhat different index of liberal parental ideology, we did not find any evidence for the following relations: (1) liberal parental ideology, civil rights reformist views of the student, and student activism or (2) liberal parental ideology, educational reform views of the student, and student activism.

In sum, our data show only the weakest links between liberal parental ideology, liberal student ideology, and activism. We would not go so far as to say the original two-variable relationship between liberal parental ideology and activism is spurious. But neither liberal nor radical ideologies of the student seem to be strong linking mechanisms between liberal parental ideology and activism.

One could speculate that liberal parental ideology may sensitize various

Table 5-4

Parents' Liberal Ideology and Student Activism, with Student's Radical Political Consciousness Controlled

Student's Radical Consciousness

Student Activism	High			Low		
	Father's Liberal Ideology			Father's Liberal Ideology		
	High	*Low*		*High*	*Low*	
Active	(17) 68%	(18) 50%	e = 18% χ^2 = N.S.	(6) 24%	(13) 19%	e = 5% χ^2 = N.S.
Total	(25) 100%	(36) 100%		(25) 100%	(67) 100%	

Student's Radical Consciousness

Student Activism	High			Low		
	Mother's Liberal Ideology			Mother's Liberal Ideology		
	High	*Low*		*High*	*Low*	
Active	(24) 73%	(19) 42%	e = 31% χ^2 = .01	(5) 21%	(14) 18%	e = 3% χ^2 = N.S.
Total	(33) 100%	(45) 100%		(24) 100%	(76) 100%	

students to issues of humanitarian concern (in contrast to more specifically political values) and that student humanitarianism may get translated into activism. We empirically tested this speculation, and we found only weak support for it. Actually, the way that liberal parental ideology mainly contributes to activism in our data is in a compensatory fashion. We found ex post facto that liberal parental ideology seems to compensate for students who are low on various unconventional cultural values in generating participation in activism—that is, liberal parental ideology and activism are positively associated mainly when the students are low on the unconventional cultural values. But liberal parental ideology does not strongly contribute to activism by the more direct linking mechanisms examined here.

Thus it appears that radical ideology of the parents is clearly more important to the development of radical political consciousness and engagement in activism than liberal parental ideology. This is an important

Table 5-5
Parents' Liberal Ideology and Student Activism

Student Activism	Parent						
	Father			Mother			
	Liberal Ideology			Liberal Ideology			
	High	Low		High	Low		
Active	(22)	(29)	e = 16%	(28)	(32)	e = 23%	
	45%	29%	χ^2 = .05	50%	27%	χ^2 = .01	
Total	(49)	(101)		(56)	(119)		
	100%	100%		100%	100%		

Table 5-6
Parents' Liberal Ideology and Student Activism, with Student's Liberal Ideology Controlled

Student Activism	Student's Liberal Ideology						
	High			Low			
	Father's Liberal Ideology			Father's Liberal Ideology			
	High	Low		High	Low		
Active	(19)	(18)	e = 11%	(3)	(11)	e = 9%	
	49%	38%	χ^2 = N.S.	30%	21%	χ^2 = N.S.	
Total	(39)	(48)		(10)	(53)		
	100%	100%		100%	100%		

Student Activism	Student's Liberal Ideology						
	High			Low			
	Mother's Liberal Ideology			Mother's Liberal Ideology			
	High	Low		High	Low		
Active	(24)	(21)	e = 24%	(4)	(11)	e = 9%	
	57%	33%	χ^2 = .02	29%	20%	χ^2 = N.S.	
Total	(42)	(63)		(14)	(56)		
	100%	100%		100%	100%		

Table 5-7
Civil Rights and Educational Reform Views: Absence of Links Between Parental Views, Student's Views, and Student Activism

I. Father's Civil Rights Views

   A. Original relationship between father's civil rights views and student activism: e = −5%.

   B. Partial tables when student's civil rights views are held constant: High, e = −6%; Low, e = 10%.

II. Mother's Civil Rights Views

   A. Original relationship between mother's civil rights views and student activism: e = 5%.

   B. Partial tables when student's civil rights views are held constant: High, e = 7%; Low, e = 2%.

III. Father's Educational Reform Views

   A. Original relationship between father's educational reform views and student activism: e = 6%.

   B. Partial tables when student's educational reform views are held constant: High, e = 7%; Low, e = −1%.

IV. Mother's Educational Reform Views

   A. Original relationship between mother's educational reform views and student activism: e = 10%.

   B. Partial tables when student's educational reform views are held constant: High, e = 0%; Low, e = 47%.

finding because various interpreters of activism such as Flacks, Lipset, and Keniston have tended to lump liberal and radical family backgrounds together. [24] Our analysis indicates the necessity to distinguish these two types of family backgrounds when analyzing the origins of radical political consciousness and student activism. At least by the end of the Sixties, liberal parental ideology did not exert a great influence over activism whereas radical, anti-capitalist ideology did.

Notes

1. Richard Flacks, "The Liberated Generation: An Exploration of the Roots of Student Protest," *The Journal of Social Issues* 23 (July 1967): 52-75. Along with Flacks, Kenneth Keniston, in such works as *Young Radicals* (New York: Harcourt, Brace & World, 1968), was an early spokesman for the left-wing socialization hypothesis. For further discussion of various types of left-wing political consciousness, and the way they are derived, see James L. Wood, *Political Consciousness and Student Activism* (Beverly Hills: Sage Publications, in press). For the question-

naire items used to measure concepts such as radical political consciousness, see Appendix C of this book.

2. Flacks, op. cit., Table 1, p. 67.

3. Ibid., pp. 66-67.

4. Ibid.

5. Ibid., p. 66.

6. Ibid., pp. 66-67. In a summary of the literature, Keniston sees more
discontinuity between left-wing students and their parents than between
conservative students and their parents. We have used the same data of
Flacks' to show both continuity and discontinuity between the generations,
as Keniston tends to suggest. Actually, Keniston suggests that the same
data could be used to examine both continuity and *conflict* between the
generations. Usually we use different data to examine actual conflict between the generations in our own study, although the same data are used at
one point to examine continuity and conflict. See Kenneth Keniston,
"Introduction" to his *Radicals and Militants: An Annotated Bibliography
of Empirical Research on Campus Unrest* (Lexington, Mass.: Lexington
Books, D.C. Heath, 1973), pp. ix-x.

7. Flacks, op. cit., p. 68.

8. Ibid.

9. For example, see Keniston, *Young Radicals,* op. cit.

10. Kenneth Keniston, "The Sources of Student Dissent," in Neil J.
Smelser and William T. Smelser, eds., *Personality and Social Systems,*
Second Edition (New York: John Wiley and Sons, 1970), p. 686.

11. Seymour Martin Lipset, *Rebellion in the University* (Boston: Little, Brown & Co., 1972), Chapter 3, pp. 80-123.

12. Report of Harris Survey of Students, May 20-28, 1970, cited in
Lipset, ibid., Table 13, p. 93.

13. R. William Cowdry and Kenneth Keniston, "The War and Military
Obligation: Attitudes, Actions and Their Consistency," mimeographed
paper, Department of Psychiatry, Yale University, 1969, cited in Lipset,
ibid., p. 101.

14. Kenneth Keniston, "Notes on Young Radicals," *Change* 1
(November-December 1969): 31, cited in Lipset, ibid., p. 103.

15. Lipset, ibid., p. 80.

16. Philip G. Altbach and David H. Kelly, *American Students: A
Selected Bibliography on Student Activism and Related Topics* (Lexington, Mass.: Lexington Books, D.C. Heath, 1973); and Keniston, *Radicals
and Militants: An Annotated Bibliography of Empirical Research on Campus Unrest,* op. cit.

17. See a discussion of these studies in Keniston, ibid., pp. 2-5, 7-8,
30-33, 164-165, 190.

18. See studies by Helen Astin discussed in Keniston, ibid., pp. 12-16. Also Feuer would reject the left wing socialization hypothesis; see Lewis S. Feuer, *The Conflict of Generations* (New York: Basic Books, 1969).

19. Keniston, *Young Radicals*, op. cit.

20. Lipset, op. cit., pp. 83, 95.

21. Flacks, op. cit., pp. 66-67.

22. Ibid., p. 66; Lipset, op. cit., p. 80.

23. See, for example, Flacks, op. cit., Table 1, p. 67; and Lipset, op. cit., Table 13, p. 93. In *Young Radicals,* op. cit., Keniston uses depth interviews, not multivariate analysis.

24. Keniston, ibid.; Lipset, op. cit.; and Flacks, op.cit.

6

A Note on Reverse Socialization and University Socialization

Reverse Socialization

Although the direction of socialization is usually from the parents to the children, in some cases the socialization process may be "reversed"[1]—that is, children may occasionally socialize their parents rather than the opposite. It has been suggested that cases exist in which parents were initially disoriented by their children's activism and radical consciousness, but later came to adopt their children's radical views.[2] Our data permit at least a limited test of these ideas.

To examine this theory of reverse socialization we are, in effect, making student's radical consciousness and student activism the independent variables and parents' radical consciousness, the dependent variable. Thus the student's ideas and actions are the primary socializing mechanisms, and the parents' ideas, the object of socialization. On one hand, we briefly examine how the student's radical *ideas* affect his parents' radical *ideas;* on the other hand, we examine how the student's radical *actions* affect his parents' radical *ideas.* Actually, the relationship between student's ideas and parents' ideas is a more obvious type of relationship than the relationship between student's actions and parents' ideas. With regard to the relationship between the ideas of student and parent, the student is seen as convincing his parents of the "correctness" of his radical ideas. But it is also possible that occasionally parents examine the "anti-Establishment" implications of their child's activism, and the examination of these implications could radicalize the parents ideologically. At most, we can only present two-variable data on these notions. However, the information to be presented should be suggestive of hypotheses that could guide further research.

When student's radical political consciousness is taken as the independent variable and parents' radical political consciousness is taken as the dependent variable, there are definite two-variable relationships. The relationship between student's radical consciousness and mother's radical consciousness is e = 23 percent, which is statistically significant by the χ^2 test at the .001 level. The relationship between student's radical consciousness and father's radical consciousness is e = 17 percent, which has a χ^2 of .01. So there is some evidence of a two-variable sort suggesting radical socialization by students of their parents. However, when student activism is taken as the independent variable, the two-variable relations are not as strong. The relationship between student activism and mother's radical political consciousness is e = 13 percent, with a χ^2 of .10. And the relationship between student activism and father's radical political consciousness is e = 10 percent, with a χ^2 of .10. It certainly would be possible, on the basis of these data, to argue that when students become ideological, they can converse with their parents and at times convert them to a radical perspective, if the parents were not originally radical politically. The effect of activism is in the same direction, but not as accentuated. It is perhaps not too surprising that there is a closer correspondence between student and parental ideology than between student action and parental ideology.[3] When these findings are combined with findings in Chapter 7 that activism seems to bring parents and children closer together, we can make a case for a rather unexpected conclusion about the contribution to improved family functioning of student activism and radical consciousness.

University Socialization

If students occasionally socialize their parents to a radical perspective, this implies that the parents were not originally radical, or that if they were radical when they were younger, they changed to a more moderate position in adulthood. Consequently, the students had to get their radical views elsewhere than from the family. The most likely alternative source of radical ideas for students is, of course, the university. One could make a good *theoretical* case for radical socialization at an institution like the University of California at Berkeley. Anyone acquainted with the "Berkeley scene" is aware of the countless political discussions that occur on campus. There are rallies, informal street arguments, politicized soap-box ministers, inside-dopesters, and so on. In various classes, social-political issues are vigorously debated. White radical students and Third World students have become alternative socialization agents in the university setting. Radical criticisms of varying levels of sophistication abound in relation to almost every public issue from the Vietnam War to pollution. Some educational scholars have even gone so far as to state the university should strongly challenge older values of students and institute more critical viewpoints among the students. Although there are many speculations about the extent the University of California at Berkeley actually changes students' values, there are not too many facts available in relation to the changes that really occur. Fortunately, our data can contribute some information on the role that U.C. Berkeley plays in changing students' views.

There is one question in the parental questionnaire that asks if U.C. Berkeley has changed the views of the students. Over a quarter of the parents of U.C. Berkeley students reported that "going to Berkeley has changed [my] sons's or daughter's basic values and outlook on life" (fathers were more likely to report these changed values than mothers). So from a descriptive standpoint there may actually be a significant *minority* of students whose values are changed by the experience of going to Berkeley. Certainly we would want to get comparable data on other colleges and universities, as well as data on young adults not in school, before we could make any more definite statements about the effects of the Berkeley campus *per se* on students' value systems. But the parental reports amount to at least suggestive evidence of the impact of the Berkeley campus on the values of an important minority of students.[4]

Less clear is the relationship between the changes in values, as reported by the parents, and student activism. There is actually a moderately strong relation of e = 23 percent, χ^2 = .01 between changed values and student activism when the student's mother reports the changed values. However, there is a much weaker relation between these variables when the father reports the changed values (e = 7 percent, and the Chi-Square is not statistically significant). The most we can say from these figures is that U.C. Berkeley seems to be a source of radical consciousness and activism for a yet-to-be-determined minority of students. The Berkeley campus seems to have some radical socializing and activizing role, but this role is by no means all-determining, as some stereotypes might have it. The U.C. Berkeley campus thus must be considered along with other determinants of radical consciousness and activism, but it must not be given a stronger role than the data suggest.

Conclusion

In sum, this brief chapter has presented limited evidence on the hypothesis of reverse socialization. We have seen some two-variable data suggesting that on occasion activists socialize their parents to radical views rather than vice versa. In this context, we have attempted to examine one extra-familial source of the students' radical views—namely, the university. We did find some support for university socialization to radical values among activists, but we also suggested caution in ascribing too much university influence in radicalizing students. Thus, the evidence of the last two chapters confirms that the socialization process for activists is usually in the expected direction from parents to child, but that occasionally the process is reversed.

Notes

1. The idea of reverse socialization was suggested to me in a private

communication by Neil J. Smelser of the Department of Sociology, University of California, Berkeley.

2. Ibid.

3. Mankoff found the closest correspondences between parents' and students' ideologies, and parents' and students' actions. See Milton L. Mankoff, *The Political Socialization of Radicals and Militants in the Wisconsin Student Movement During the 1960's,* unpublished Ph.D. dissertation, Department of Sociology, University of Wisconsin, Madison, Wisconsin, 1969.

4. Robert H. Somers and his colleagues at the Institute for Research in Social Behavior, The Claremont Hotel, Berkeley, California 94705, are conducting a longitudinal study of the U. C. Berkeley campus. This study will provide much more information on the impact of the University of California at Berkeley on students' values. For an earlier study of the impact of U. C. Berkeley on liberal political values of the student, see Henry C. Finney, "Political Libertarianism at Berkeley: An Application of Perspectives from the New Student Left," *The Journal of Social Issues* 27, No. 1 (1971): 35-61. The data on which Finney's study is based were collected at two time periods: 1959 and 1961. There have been some other discussions in recent years that have systematically attempted to determine the impact of colleges and universities on students' social and political views. For example, see Kenneth A. Feldman and Theodore M. Newcomb, *The Impact of College on Students* (San Francisco, California: Jossey-Bass, 1969); Volume I: *An Analysis of Four Decades of Research;* Volume II: *Summary Tables.*

7 The Conflict of Generations

Introduction

One of the major alternatives to an approach focusing on shared radical values between activists and their parents is the approach to activism centering on the conflict between the generations. Richard Flacks, an adherent to the approach advocating value continuity between the generations, recently addressed the conflict of generations approach and explicitly rejected it. In his book *Youth and Social Change,* Flacks states: "Generational conflict expressed through collective action is neither inevitable nor the result of repressed Oedipal impulses."[1] Nevertheless, the idea that the students of the 1960s were in revolt against their parents received much attention and certainly deserves an empirical test. In fact, it can be shown that the approaches focusing on value continuity and generational conflict are a good deal more compatible than is usually felt to be the case. The dual set of findings on value continuity and generational conflict, of course, support our middle-range theory of activism discussed in Chapter 2.

Probably the most famous proponent of the conflict of generations approach to activism is Lewis Feuer.[2] As a result, this chapter examines his theory in detail. We first examine the logical structure of his argument, and then we attempt to empirically test at least part of this theory. Although there are a variety of logical and methodological flaws in his approach to activism, there is also empirical support for his contention that activists have had conflictual relations with their parents. However, activists do not reject their parents' radical political values, and participation in activism actually improves family relations. Feuer's approach would not predict either of these results.

Feuer's Theory of Generational Conflict

Feuer's notion of a conflict between the generations is complex and needs to be spelled out. Here, we isolate the major types of generational conflicts that Feuer believes are determinants of student activism and then we develop empirical measures of at least some of these forms of conflicts in order to see the empirical association of the conflicts with student activism.

Among the various ways that Feuer uses the term "conflict of generations" are the following:

1. Hostile parent-child relationships;
2. Actual conflict and struggle between parents and children;
3. Distant relations between parents and children;
4. Rejection of parental values by their children;
5. "De-authoritization" of the older generation by the younger generation;
6. Alienation from the older generation by the younger generation;
7. Unresolved Oedipal crises on the part of the younger generation;
8. Subjection of the younger generation to harsh childrearing practices;
9. Emotional rebellion on the part of the younger generation against the older generation (which is distinct from more "rational" rebellions of other groups such as workers who rebel against long hours).[3]

Each of these elements of the conflict of generations has the same function for Feuer—that is, each leads members of the younger generation to protest against the older generation. Here we are interested in one specific type of protest—namely, political protest (which is also Feuer's primary interest).

Feuer tries to explain student protests on a universal basis. Instead of focusing on any given protest such as the Free Speech Movement, he tries to explain all student protests at all times and places throughout history. He feels he can understand protests at such a general level because of the universality of the conflict of generations. The young, he tries to argue, always seem to be in rebellion against the old due to such factors as hostility of the young against the old, harsh childrearing practices by the old in relation to their children, and so forth. An examination of a few of Feuer's discussions of student protests should illustrate how he uses the concept "conflict of generations."

In discussing Gavrilo Princip, who with two other students assassinated the Archduke Franz Ferdinand in June 1914 to set off World War I, Feuer says:

. . . several months of psychiatric interviews with Princip as well as the testimony of his close friend show him to have been laboring under the severe strain of generational conflict—intense love for his mother which he is described as "confessing," combined with hostility toward his father.[4]

Furthermore, Feuer points out:

His fantasy life was filled with images of assassination. Gavrilo Princip acted out the heroic politics of his struggle with his parents on the stage of history and imposed his pattern of self-destruction on most of Europe and the rest of the world.[5]

Feuer's analysis of Princip sounds very much like Princip was motivated by an unresolved Oedipus complex. He was very attached to his mother and antagonistic toward his father; the Archduke served as a father-surrogate, whom Princip killed in order to symbolically kill his own father. Hall speaks of the Oedipus complex:

Prior to the emergence of the phallic period, the boy loves his mother and identifies with his father. When the sexual urge increases, the boy's love for his mother becomes more incestuous and as a result he becomes jealous of his rival, the father. This state of affairs in which the boy craves exclusive sexual possession of the mother and feels antagonistic toward his father is called the *Oedipus complex*. Oedipus was a prominent figure in Greek mythology who killed his father and married his mother.[6]

For most males, the Oedipus complex gets resolved by the son repressing his sexual desires for the mother and identifying with the father, as well as forming his superego.[7] However, successful resolution of the Oedipus complex does not always occur, with the result of continued hostility toward the father by the son and continued love of the mother. Authority figures can take the place of the father symbolically and therefore be the target of hostility, including political revolution, on the part of the son.[8]

The Oedipus complex can be used to understand the politics of female students as well as male students. In discussing the Oedipus complex of females, Hall says:

As with the boy, the girl's first love object, apart from love of her own body (narcissism), is the mother, but unlike the case of the boy there is not likely to be an early identification with the father. When the girl discovers that she does not possess the noticeable external genitals of the male, she feels castrated. She blames her mother for this condition and the cathexis for the mother is thereby weakened. . . . in the girl the castration complex (penis envy) is responsible for the introduction of the Oedipus complex. She loves her father and is jealous of her mother. Although the female Oedipus complex is not as likely to disappear as the male's, it does become weaker by virtue of maturation, and the impossibility of possessing the father. Identifications then take the place of object-cathexes.[9]

As with males, some females do not adequately resolve the Oedipus complex, and as a result continue their hostility to their mothers and their love for their fathers. Feuer picks up on this theme in discussing former student activist and accused atomic spy, Ethel Rosenberg. Feuer says that "Ethel hated her devout, illiterate mother, and modeled herself, in every way, to be her opposite."[10] Similarly, her husband Julius Rosenberg—well-known student activist at City College in New York in the 1930s, as well as accused atomic spy—had conflictual relations with his father. Feuer says that by 1945 Rosenberg's father refused to see his son for such reasons as Rosenberg's "intolerance to Trotskyites [Julius was a member of the Young Communist League] and for forgetting that America was a 'free country'."[11]

Furthermore, in trying to understand the German Youth Movement, Feuer cites with approval psychiatrist Karl Stern:

For some unknown reason, the relationship between generations, particularly that between father and son, seems much more problematic in Germany than in Anglo-Saxon countries. [In schools] the teacher was always a victim of aggressions and hostility.[12]

German youth after World War I not only had conflictual relations with their parents. Feuer also argues that many in the Youth Movement rejected their parents' values. Feuer again quotes Stern in relation to members of the German Youth Movement:

All of them had one thing in common: a rebellious attitude against their parents' generation, or at least against the mode of living of that generation. There was a sort of ascetic protest against everything "bourgeois"—no drinking, no smoking, no smart clothes.[13]

This rejection of parental values on the part of student activists occurs, in Feuer's view, for left-wing students as well as the right-wing German students discussed by Stern. Left-wing students are seen by Feuer as rejecting middle-class values of their parents when their parents hold these values; as rejecting left-wing (i.e., "old" left-wing) values of their parents when their parents hold these values; and as rejecting liberal values when their parents hold these values. At one point Feuer even warns the current Russian regime against potential rebellion of Russian students. (However, he later applauds certain Russian students who defy the current regime.)[14]

Feuer quotes Free Speech Movement activist Gerald Rosenfield to the effect that the FSM was "a revolt against the values and mores with which our parents had constructed their own self-images and life styles."[15] Furthermore, Feuer states that Berkeley activists "rejected any prolongation among themselves of the disputes of the Old Leftists, the 'distrust and prejudice based on the experiences of their fathers.' . . . They sought to preserve their generational unity, and believed firmly that the bond of youthful idealism would surmount ideological differences."[16] Finally, Feuer states that Professor Morris R.Cohen attracted great animosity from left-wing Jewish students in the 1930s in New York because:

He was the first of the fathers to have won recognition in the American academic and liberal world. In an atmosphere of generational conflict, he tended therefore to become the surrogate object for vehement attack.[17]

Thus, Feuer is arguing that almost irrespective of the content of the values, student activists reject their parents' values and that this rejection is a prime motivation for their participation in instances of student activism.

Still another aspect of the conflict of generations in Feuer's book is harsh childrearing experiences endured by activists. Feuer points out that a well-known student activist in his day, Mao Tse-tung, was treated severely by his father:

Mao's childhood and adolescence had been years marked by perpetual conflict with his father, a rice merchant and "severe taskmaster," who frequently beat Mao and his brothers, exploited him as well as his laborers, and gave him the most meager food.[18]

However, Mao had good relations with his mother: "Mao was drawn to his mother, who gave food to the poor during famines."[19] Feuer concludes:

Mao's conflict with his father and its primacy as a motivation for his political ideas were typical of the Chinese students who emerged with him as leaders in the Communist movement.[20]

Feuer is not overly clear about how these various aspects of generational conflict relate to each other. Rather, his model seems to be that all elements of generational conflict propel students to become involved in student or youth movements that are antagonistic to the established social order. If there is an "underlying" variable in his system from which the other variables are derived, it is Freud's idea of an unresolved Oedipus complex discussed above. Feuer notes that "the conflict of generations . . . derives from deep, unconscious sources."[21] Also, he defines a student movement in part as an "emotional rebellion."[22] And, with regard to the Russian student movement, Feuer says:

. . . the acts of Czar-killing and self-killing . . . brought into the domain of Russian politics the psychology of sons destroying their fathers, re-enacting on a national political scale the dramatic emotions portrayed by Freud in *Totem and Taboo*, the revolt and guilt of the primal sons.[23]

There are several logical, methodological, and empirical difficulties with Feuer's study. For example, his use of very selective illustrations is not the most systematic evidence that could be gathered to test his propositions about student activism. One book that was very available to him that did try to get systematic data on activism, *The Berkeley Student Revolt,* does not get cited by Feuer.[24] Amidst the impressive array of obscure references Feuer does cite, this is not a minor omission, especially since some of the data in *The Berkeley Student Revolt* do not necessarily support his interpretation of activism.[25] Also, his use of Freud is very *ad hoc;* he brings in Freudian concepts where they support his argument, but he does not really try to systematically test Freud's theory. Also, as the student movements become more well-known, it is apparent that he periodically overstates the case. It is much easier, for example, to appraise his interpretation of the Free Speech Movement than the Bosnian or even Russian student movements. But his overstatement of facts and interpretations of better-known instances of student activism sheds some doubt on his selection of facts and interpretations of lesser-known instances of activism.

For example, Feuer clearly would like to show that Mario Savio had conflicting relations with his father. However, Feuer is forced to admit that Savio actually had very good relations with his father.[26] But this fact does not prevent Feuer from implying that Savio was filled with antagonism toward his father. Feuer argues that the university provided a substitute target for Savio's generational hatred.[27] But on closer inspection this is an example of circular reasoning. Feuer has no basis to imply that Savio hated his father other than the fact Savio engaged in student activism. However, he also explains Savio's activism by his hatred for his father. Thus, activism both indicates father-hatred and is a result of father-hatred—a clear case of circular reasoning. Finally, Feuer states that this was the case "with so many [Berkeley] student activists."[28] For this last assertion Feuer presents no evidence. Other examples could be provided, and it is not unfair to say Feuer periodically overstates the case about the reasons why students engage in activism.

Furthermore, the time order of Feuer's variables is not always clear, which sheds some doubt on his theory of activism. For example, in the Rosenberg example cited above, it is not clear whether Julius Rosenberg started having poor relations with his father before or after he was a student activist in New York. Presumably, if Rosenberg had good relations with his father at the time he was an activist (and he had good relations with his father for a long period of time before their estrangement), then there would not be much ground to say father-hatred led to Rosenberg's activism. Finally, Feuer admits that it is possible to level the charge of "reductionism" against his approach—that is, students are not really motivated by ideals and ideology when they engage in politics, only by generational hatred. Feuer does not exactly deny the charge but instead attempts to defend his approach by showing how it explains the supposed violence and extremism of student movements directed against a hated older generation.[29] It is certainly possible to list more deficiencies with Feuer's study (one reviewer felt the book showed more about Feuer than about student activism). Ever since the book was published (and prior to its publication with his articles expounding the same theme), Feuer has been the target of criticism.[30] Much of this criticism has been analytical, with only occasional empirical testing of his ideas.[31] At this point, we can take some of Feuer's ideas and attempt to test them with our data in order to see whether this overall viewpoint has stronger empirical support than Feuer himself provided.

An Empirical Test of Feuer's Theory

Various aspects of the family relations of student activists, especially the childrearing practices and relations reported by the parents in this study, can be applied to Feuer's theory. The data obtained from these parents would presumably get around the criticism of collecting family data from the activists themselves—that is, if the activists actually did have a lot of antagonism to their parents in the Freudian sense (or otherwise), they might well repress the poor relations and thereby bias any results obtained from them. Their parents presumably would not have as much "stake" in avoiding a discussion of poor relations with their children. As a matter of fact, the students, when asked about their family relations, tended to report less family difficulties than their parents on the one family-relations item in the student questionnaire. (However, no parents admitted they had "no relationship" at all with their children, whereas a few students reported this.) Fortunately, there was another study of Berkeley activists that examined parent-child relations from the standpoint of the student. That study used the same Q-Sort methods employed here and came to the same conclusions about the conflictual relations activists had with their parents.[32] Clearly this other study (which was even carried out by the same investigator who collected the Berkeley data analyzed throughout this book) lends strong support to our own conclusions.

The data collected in our Berkeley study from both the students and the parents tend to show a positive relation between family conflict and student activism—that is, the worse relations a student had with his or her parents, the more likely he or she was to be an activist. This conclusion will have to be examined in light of the various indices of family relations we have, but it seems to be an assertion that covers quite a bit of the data.

Table 7-1 shows essentially no original relationship between activism and parental hostility to the student during his or her childhood (e = 1 percent for fathers and e = 3 percent for mothers). However, we know that at times an initial two-variable relationship may have no statistical association because other positive and negative associations with the dependent variable cancel each other out. To some extent this is the case with parental hostility and student activism. In order to roughly approximate a test of Feuer's ideas, sex will be introduced as a control variable for the original relationship.[33] For Feuer's Oedipal crisis ideas to have some substantiation, male activists would have to have had poor relations with their fathers, but good relations with their mothers. On the other hand, female activists would have to have had good relations with their fathers, but poor relations with their mothers.

When student's sex is introduced as a third variable (Table 7-2), at least part of the predictions based on Freudian theory are borne out. Fathers

Table 7-1
Parents' Hostility to Child During Childhood and Student Activism

	Parent		
	Father		
Student Activism	Hostility		
	High	Low	
Active	(21) 39%	(30) 38%	e = 1% χ^2 = N.S.
Total	(54) 100%	(80) 100%	
	Mother		
Student Activism	Hostility		
	High	Low	
Active	(22) 38%	(36) 35%	e = 3% χ^2 = N.S.
Total	(58) 100%	(102) 100%	

tended to be somewhat hostile to male activists but were not hostile to
female activists. This would be predicted from Feuer's Freudian approach
to student activism. However, when these relationships for mothers are
examined, predictions from Feuer's theory are not borne out. The greater
the hostility by the mother, the greater the likelihood the son would be an
activist. Also, there was an inverse relationship between activism for
females and maternal hostility—that is, the more likely the mother was
hostile to her daughter during childhood, the less likely the daughter would
be an activist. In fact, for both fathers and mothers there is a positive
relation between hostility and activism for sons, but an inverse relation
between hostility and activism for daughters. Thus, the Freudian approach
of Feuer receives some confirmation by these tables, especially for the
father's relationship with his children. But the Freudian approach does not
receive this type of confirmation when mothers are considered. In fact, just
the opposite findings occur when mother's relations with her children are
considered. Further examination of the data helps evaluate the Freudian
approach to activism developed by Feuer, as well as a more general

Table 7-2
Parents' Hostility to Child During Childhood and Student Activism, with Student's Sex Controlled

	Sex of Student					
	Male			Female		
Student Activism	Father's Hostility			Father's Hostility		
	High	Low		High	Low	
Active	(15) 47%	(18) 38%	e = 9% χ² = N.S.	(6) 27%	(12) 36%	e = −9% χ² = N.S.
Total	(32) 100%	(47) 100%		(22) 100%	(33) 100%	

	Sex of Student					
	Male			Female		
Student Activism	Mother's Hostility			Mother's Hostility		
	High	Low		High	Low	
Active	(16) 50%	(20) 35%	e = 15% χ² = N.S.	(6) 23%	(16) 36%	e = −13% χ² = N.S.
Total	(32) 100%	(57) 100%		(26) 100%	(45) 100%	

approach to student activism stressing family conflicts and poor relations *without* regard to the Oedipal situation.

Another meaning of the conflict of generations used by Feuer refers to actual conflict and struggle between parents and their children. Do activists tend to come from backgrounds where parents report a high degree of conflict during childrearing? As Table 7-3 shows, there is a strong original relationship between conflict in childrearing and activism for both parents. However, when sex is introduced as a third control variable (Table 7-4), the original relations change in exactly the opposite direction than would be predicted by Feuer's Freudian approach to activism—that is, the original relation between father's report of conflict and activism decreases when the son is considered, but increases when the daughter is considered. Similarly, the original relation between mother's report of conflict and activism decreases when the daughter is considered, but increases when the son is considered. Thus, our rough test of the Oedipal approach to

Table 7-3
Parents' Report of Conflict During Childrearing and Student Activism

Student Activism	Parent Father Conflict		
	High	Low	
Active	(16) 76%	(30) 29%	e = 47% χ^2 = .001
Total	(21) 100%	(102) 100%	

Student Activism	Mother Conflict		
	High	Low	
Active	(14) 67%	(40) 32%	e = 35% χ^2 = .01
Total	(21) 100%	(127) 100%	

activism does not receive much confirmation when conflictual parent-child relations are examined. Nevertheless, the more general approach to student activism that stresses conflict between parents and children, but which does not stress the Oedipus complex, does receive strong confirmation in these data.

We have three measures of the next meaning of the conflict of generations—namely, distant relations between parents and children. We have measures of close or distant relations reported by both parents and children, and the parents' report of their relations with their children at two time periods, the present and during childrearing. The student's report is only of present relations. The findings do not exhibit a consistent support or rejection of the Freudian approach to student activism as we have been trying to test it. For example, there is almost no original relation between father's report of close or distant relations during childrearing and activism (e = 2 percent). Yet, when sex is introduced as a third variable, this original relation increases to e = 16 percent for females and reverses to e = −8 percent for males—that is, the father was likely to have close relations with

Table 7-4
Parents' Report of Conflict During Childrearing and Student Activism, with Student's Sex Controlled

	Student's Sex					
	Male			Female		
Student Activism	Father's Conflict			Father's Conflict		
	High	Low		High	Low	
Active	(10) 71%	(18) 31%	e = 40% χ² = .01	(6) 86%	(12) 27%	e = 59% χ² = .01
Total	(14) 100%	(58) 100%		(7) 100%	(44) 100%	

	Student's Sex					
	Male			Female		
Student Activism	Mother's Conflict			Mother's Conflict		
	High	Low		High	Low	
Active	(8) 100%	(26) 35%	e = 65% χ² = .001	(6) 46%	(14) 26%	e = 20% χ² = N.S.
Total	(8) 100%	(74) 100%		(13) 100%	(53) 100%	

his activist daughter, but distant relations with his activist son, just as the Freudian approach would predict. However, when the student's relationship with the mother is considered, the original relation is mildly negative (e = −7 percent). This decreases to e = −1 percent when activist daughters are considered but slightly increases to e = −10 percent when activist sons are considered—that is, activist sons are more likely to have distant relations with their mothers than activist daughters, which would not be predicated by the Freudian approach to activism. Nevertheless, when all three measures of closeness or distance of parent-child relations are taken into account, there is at least a moderate tendency for activists to have distant relations with their parents.

Tables 10-2 and 10-4 measure the extent to which harsh childrearing methods relate to activism. This, of course, is still another way Feuer indicated the conflict of generations. It seems that only for Catholic fathers is there a positive relation between harsh punishment during childrearing and student activism (this also holds for fathers of "Other" religions, although the cases are very few for this category). So there is not too much evidence for this type of generational conflict and activism.

Similarly, contrary to the previous findings on the conflict of generations is the finding that parental affection during childrearing seems to be positively related to student activism. For example, there is a relationship of $e = 21$ percent between father's report of affection to his children during childhood and activism when the son is considered. The only reversal of this relationship is for fathers and their daughters—father's report of affection is negatively related to activism when daughters are considered.

Even though these findings on harsh childrearing and affection during childrearing seem to go contrary to the previous findings on the conflict of generations and activism, we think the previous findings are sufficiently consistent to assert an overall relation between conflictual parent-child relations and activism. There is less support for the more specifically Freudian approach that was tested by holding sex constant for each of the measures of the conflict of generations. Nevertheless, the Freudian approach did receive some confirmation. In sum, we can conclude that the more likely a student is to have had conflictual relations with his or her parents, the more likely it is that he or she will be a student activist.

There is one final meaning of the conflict of generations, which must be considered, that is at a different level of analysis than the types of conflicts we have been discussing. This is Feuer's contention that student activists reject their parents' values almost irrespective of the content of those values. Earlier we discussed a theory of activism that stressed a continuity of values between the student activists and their parents. Our data indicated that radically conscious activists tended to be children of radically conscious parents. In addition, we found a positive relationship between parental liberalism and student activism, although we did not feel that student liberalism was a strong link between parental liberalism and activism. Thus, there is possible support for Feuer's position when he says student activists have rejected their parents' liberal views (our evidence does not show rejection; it only shows student liberalism is not a clear linking mechanism). But Feuer's position must be rejected when radically conscious parents are considered; our data indicate an acceptance of a radical perspective by student activists whose parents are radically politically conscious. So it seems that students can have conflictual and even hostile relations with their parents but nevertheless accept their political viewpoints. Thus, approaches to activism stressing conflict and continuity between the generations turn out to be more compatible than previously believed by many analysts of activism.

It is important to interpret why these theories are at least partly compatible. These two theories have stronger empirical support than other middle-range theories tested in this study. Hence, some type of synthesis of the two approaches to activism could provide an improved understanding of the origins of activism.

We suggest that these findings point to the conclusion previously discussed. Many activists can be seen as acting out radical political values derived from their parents' radical political or culturally unconventional values.[34] However, many activists come into conflict with their parents because of the activists' perception that their parents have failed to live up to their own politically radical or culturally unconventional values. At one point in "The Liberated Generation" Flacks suggests this interpretation of activism. He notes that "An additional source of strain [on activists] is generated when these young people perceive a fundamental discrepancy between the values espoused by their parents and the style of life actually practiced by them.[35] The activists, according to Flacks, perceive their parents as hypocritical when they "express liberal or intellectual values while appearing to their children as acquisitive or self-interested."[36] Here Flacks refers to liberal rather than radical values, but he often merges the two types of political values as leftist values in general. But it is clear that he sees the potential for conflict between the generations over the failure of parents to live up to their own political or cultural ideals, although Flacks does not generally emphasize generational conflict. We have previously presented qualitative data on activists' perception that their parents have failed to realize their own political and cultural values. Thus, we argue that this type of feeling on the part of activists toward their parents makes intelligible the dual support in our data for approaches stressing both continuity and conflict between the generations.

The idea that activists act out radical ideology derived from parental values, yet come into conflict with the parents, is compatible with a central aspect of Freud's theory of the Oedipus complex. However, it is *not* the aspect that Feuer emphasizes. In *Totem and Taboo,* Freud emphasizes the importance of the sons' *ambivalent* feelings about their father.[37] They hated him for his repressions against them, but they also loved, admired, and identified with him.[38] They wanted to be like him. As such, the sons could be seen as accepting the father's values, but coming into conflict with him nevertheless (although the conflict in *Totem and Taboo* was over his repressions, not over his failure to live up to his own ideals). In interpreting Freud, Feuer mainly emphasizes the *negative* aspects of the sons' feelings about their father.[39] He argues that the sons reject the father on all counts. By de-emphasizing the positive feelings of the sons about their father, Feuer thereby de-emphasizes the ambivalence the sons felt toward their father, which is central to Freud's thought. We do not have quantitative data on ambivalent feelings of activists toward their parents. But the qualitative data already presented suggest that ambivalence should be taken into account in understanding activists' relationships with their parents.

Participation in Student Activism

Once a student participates in student activism, the student's relationship with his or her parents actually improves. There does not seem to be an exact theory of how activism affects parent-child relationships, but there is at least a general impression that activism worsens these relationships. Our data show just the opposite. Forty-five percent of the fathers in this study reported closer relations with their activist children as compared to 26 percent of the fathers who reported no recent change in the relationship and 28 percent who reported more distant relations. The original figure of 45 percent increases to 53 percent of the fathers who reported closer relations with their activist sons. Similarly, 54 percent of the mothers reported closer relations with their activist children as compared to 14 percent who reported no recent change in the relationship and 32 percent who reported more distant relations. The original figure of 54 percent increases to 64 percent of the mothers who reported closer relations with their activist daughters.

This unanticipated finding of improved family relations and activism is consistent with our argument of value continuity between the generations. We have stated that activists often act out the values of their parents. Thus, it is possible that the ideologically radical parents in the sample approved of their children's engagement in student activism because the students were acting out parental values.[40]

More generally, participation in student activism may open channels of communication between parents and children—especially between parents and children of the same sex—that previously were closed. Engagement in activism could bring up topics of basic values on the part of parents and children that were not otherwise discussed between the generations. This could, of course, happen in families where the parents are ideologically radical or in families where the parents are not. The effect of activism in opening channels of communication would be the same irrespective of the ideological dispositions of the parents. There is even further confirmation for this viewpoint when we recall that activists tended to have strained relations with their parents. The combined findings suggest that prior to the engagement in activism there was conflict between activists and their parents. But the engagement in activism actually improved relations between the generations because it opened channels of communication between the generations.

Conclusion

The conflict of generations approach to activism thus receives some confirmation in the Berkeley study. Many activists had conflictual relations with their parents, as Feuer would predict. However, the conflict between the generations is not nearly a total explanation of student activism, as Feuer suggests. Instead, we have shown the utility of an approach that combines the insights concerning the conflict of generations with findings about the basic value continuity between the generations of radically conscious families.[41] We have even provided additional indirect support of our argument by showing that family relations improve when the students engage in activism—that is, many parents approve of their children acting out values they share. Thus, both conflict and continuity between the generations exist in families of activists, and our middle-range theory of activism is able to explain this dual set of findings.

Notes

1. Richard Flacks, *Youth and Social Change* (Chicago: Markham Publishing Co., 1971), p. 89.

2. Lewis S. Feuer, *The Conflict of Generations* (New York: Basic Books, 1969).

3. See Ibid., pp. 7-9, 11, 28, 32-33, 182-3, 288, 369, 470, 473, Chapter 10, pp. 501-34, especially pp. 515, 523-4, 530-1.

4. Ibid., pp. 7-8.

5. Ibid., p. 8.

6. Calvin S. Hall, *A Primer of Freudian Psychology* (New York: The World Publishing Co., A Mentor Book, published by The New American Library, 1954, 1961), p. 109.

7. Ibid., pp. 109-10.

8. Freud was only occasionally explicit as to how his theory of personality related to politics. See, for example, Sigmund Freud, *Totem and Taboo,* authorized translation by James Strachey, (New York: W.W. Norton & Co., 1950); and Sigmund Freud, *Group Psychology and the Analysis of the Ego,* translated by James Strachey (New York: Bantam Books, 1921, 1960). Feuer, of course, tries to spell out some of the implications of Freud's theory for the understanding of student politics. For a more general attempt to spell out the implications of Freud's theory for politics, see Philip Rieff, *Freud: The Mind of the Moralist* (Garden City, N. Y.: Anchor Books, 1959, 1961).

9. Hall, op. cit., p. 111.

10. Feuer, op. cit., p. 369.

11. Ibid.

12. Karl Stern cited in Feuer, ibid., p. 288.

13. Ibid.

14. See Feuer, ibid., pp. 288, 356, 470, 473, 531.

15. Gerald Rosenfield cited in Feuer, ibid., p. 473.

16. Feuer, op. cit., p. 470.

17. Ibid., p. 356.

18. Ibid., p. 182.

19. Ibid.

20. Ibid., p. 183.

21. Ibid., p. 10.

22. Ibid., p. 11.

23. Ibid., p. 162.

24. Seymour Martin Lipset and Sheldon S. Wolin, eds., *The Berkeley Student Revolt* (Garden City, N. Y.: Anchor Books, 1965).

25. See especially the studies by Robert H. Somers, "The Mainsprings of the Rebellion: A Survey of Berkeley Students in November, 1964," in ibid., p. 530-57; and Glen Lyonns, "The Police Car Demonstration: A Survey of Participants," in ibid., pp. 519-30.

26. Feuer, op. cit., p. 444.

27. Ibid.

28. Ibid.

29. See Feuer, ibid., pp. 530-1. However, on pp. viii-ix, Feuer states that he hopes his book will help reverse what he considers to be negative, even "demonic," trends of student movements. He likens his effort in this book to that of Robert Michels, who described the "iron law of oligarchy" in organizations yet hoped his book might help reverse the trend.

30. See, for example, Richard Flacks, "Review Article: Feuer's *Conflict of Generations*," *Journal of Social History* 4 (Winter 1970-71): 141-53; Howard Zinn, "Young Demons," a review of Lewis S. Feuer, *The Conflict of Generations,* reference not cited on my copy of Zinn's review; Frederick Crews, "The Radical Students," book review of Lewis S. Feuer, *The Conflict of Generations,* and two other books—William M. Birenbaum, *Overlive: Power, Poverty, and the University,* (Delacorte), and Immanuel Wallerstein, *University in Turmoil: The Politics of Change* (Atheneum), *The New York Review of Books,* Vol. XII, No. 8 April 24, 1969, pp. 29-34; Gerald Rosenfield, "Generational Revolt and the Free Speech Movement (Part 2)," *Liberation* X, No. 10 (January 1966); see also

the many references of criticism of Feuer's theory prior to the publication of his book that Feuer himself cites in Feuer, op. cit., footnote 85 of Chapter Nine, pp. 497-8.

31. An exception is Jeanne H. Block, Norma Haan, and M. Brewster Smith, "Socialization Correlates of Student Activism," *The Journal of Social Issues* XXV, No. 4 (1969): 143-77. These investigators found that activists had conflictual relations with their parents. Similarly, Mankoff found rebellion from parents among activists. See Milton L. Mankoff, *The Political Socialization of Radicals and Militants in the Wisconsin Student Movement During the 1960s,* unpublished Ph.D. dissertation, Department of Sociology, University of Wisconsin, Madison, Wisconsin, 1969. However, Pinkney found that civil rights activists did not have highly conflictual relations with their parents. See Alphonso Pinkney, *The Committed: White Activists in the Civil Rights Movement* (New Haven: College and University Press, 1968), pp. 60-62.

32. See Block, Haan, and Smith, op. cit. These investigators had a different sample of Berkeley activists than we have.

33. This idea was suggested to me in a private communication by Neil J. Smelser, Department of Sociology, University of California, Berkeley. However, it is clear that my data cannot test all of the subtleties of a Freudian approach to politics, as Smelser has also pointed out.

34. We develop in Chapter 8 how parents' unconventional cultural values can be a source of radical political consciousness among student activists.

35. Richard Flacks, "The Liberated Generation: An Exploration of the Roots of Student Protest," *The Journal of Social Issues* 23 (July 1967): 61.

36. Ibid.

37. Freud, *Totem and Taboo,* op. cit., pp. 128-61.

38. Ibid., p. 143.

39. See, for example, Feuer's discussion of the negative aspects of Freud's *Totem and Taboo* in Feuer, op. cit., p. 162.

40. Keniston even notes that activists' parents may be "secretly proud" that their children are acting out values that the parents have only "given lip service to." See Kenneth Keniston, "The Sources of Student Dissent," in Neil J. Smelser and William T. Smelser, eds., *Personality and Social Systems,* Second Edition (New York: John Wiley and Sons, 1970), p. 686.

41. In the last chapter we will give even a broader interpretation to activism which puts many middle-range theories—including ours—into a larger perspective.

8

Cultural and Social Alienation

Introduction

Theorists such as Flacks and Keniston have repeatedly argued that the family backgrounds of activists are not only distinct politically but culturally as well.[1] Activists are said to be socialized in families that emphasize rather unconventional cultural values, such as expressivity of impulses, humanitarianism, cooperation, romanticism, and intellectualism. These cultural values are seen as distinct from the more conventional Protestant Ethic values that tend to characterize families of non-activists.

There are two ways in which these unconventional cultural values are seen as linked to student activism. First, the student is seen to internalize the same cultural values as his or her parents, and these cultural values are translated directly into activism. The other formulation sees the student developing *political consciousness* as a result of being socialized in a family with distinct *cultural* values, and this political consciousness is then translated into activism. There is a good deal more support in our study for the approach linking cultural values of the parents, political consciousness of the student, and activism, than the approach linking cultural values of the parents, cultural values of the student, and activism.

One of the main purposes of this chapter is to examine a theory of activism that involves the cultural alienation of activists. Since cultural values, such as romanticism, are distinct from Protestant Ethic values, it is possible to develop a theory of student protest based on cultural, as distinguished from political, alienation. This is just what authors such as Roszak try to do.[2] Roszak argues that New Left student activists have much in common with the more obvious cultural rebels, the "hippies." This is the case because he feels both the New Leftists and the hippies have a shared high evaluation for the individual and a disdain for technological values of an industrial civilization.[3] In contrast to this position, others have argued that New Left activists want to *own* Western civilization; only the hippies want to *drop out* of technological society entirely.[4] But the idea that activists are cultural rebels, which has received attention in the literature and in the mass media, can be empirically examined with our Berkeley data.

The approach to activism that focuses on links between distinct cultural values of the parents, political consciousness of the student, and activism does *not* emphasize cultural alienation of activists. Instead it shows how political consciousness—especially radical political consciousness—emerges in families that are culturally unconventional. In this formulation, the students are seen as radically conscious, not culturally alienated. In contrast, the approach that focuses on links between distinct cultural values of the parents, distinct cultural values of the student, and activism *does* emphasize cultural alienation of activists. Again, there is much more support for the approach that focuses on the radical consciousness of the students than on the students' cultural alienation. This support, in turn, provides important evidence for our argument that many activists are acting out radical values derived from their parents' radical political *or* culturally unconventional values. Finally, this chapter briefly looks at one other form of alienation that some feel is linked to activism—namely, social alienation.

Unconventional Cultural Values and Activism

Among the specific values that have been seen as influencing activism are the following: romanticism (esthetic and emotional sensitivity), intellectualism (concern with ideas), humanitarianism (concern with the plight of others in society), cooperation (antagonism to competition), and expressivity of impulses (relaxed attitude toward conventional moral inhibitions).[5] Each of these cultural values is thought to contribute independently to the participation in activism.

Humanitarianism

The argument for direct cultural links between parents and their activist children is stated here in terms amenable to testing by the elaboration schema, as was the case for political values. First, the cultural value of humanitarianism is examined and then the other cultural values. Humanitarian values of the parents is the independent variable, student activism is the dependent variable, and student humanitarianism is the intervening variable that links the independent and dependent variables. Student activists are seen as adequately socialized to humanitarian values, which later get translated into student political activism. Thus, the humanitarianism of the student is seen to interpret the relationship between humanitarian values of the parents and student activism.

According to the rules for interpretation, there should be an original relationship between parental humanitarianism and student activism. Then this original relationship should become reduced in all partial tables when

Table 8-1
Parents' Humanitarianism and Student Activism

	Parent		
	Father		
Student Activism	Humanitarianism		
	High	Low	
Active	(38) 34%	(8) 35%	e = −1% χ^2 = N.S.
Total	(110) 100%	(23) 100%	
	Mother		
Student Activism	Humanitarianism		
	High	Low	
Active	(52) 39%	(5) 22%	e = 17% χ^2 = N.S.
Total	(134) 100%	(23) 100%	

the third variable of student humanitarianism is held constant. When the third variable of student humanitarianism was held constant, the results did not come out as expected. Furthermore, the results are so different for fathers and mothers that they must be discussed separately. As Tables 8-1 and 8-2 show, there is essentially no original relationship between father's humanitarian values and student activism, and there remains no relationship even when student humanitarianism is controlled. Thus, father's socialization of humanitarian values does not seem to have any bearing on the likelihood of student activism.

There is, however, a moderate original relationship between mother's humanitarian values and student activism, as Table 8-1 indicates. However, when the third variable of student humanitarianism was held constant, a specification of the original relationship occurred instead of the anticipated interpretation—that is, the original relation between mother's humanitarianism and activism was e = 17 percent, which increased to e = 29 percent under the condition of high student humanitarianism, but reversed to e = −18 percent under the condition of low student humanitarianism.

Table 8-2
Parents' Humanitarianism and Student Activism, with Student's Humanitarianism Controlled

Student's Humanitarianism

	High			Low		
Student Activism	*Father's Humanitarianism*			*Father's Humanitarianism*		
	High	Low		High	Low	
Active	(29)	(6)	e = 1%	(9)	(2)	e = −2%
	36%	35%	χ^2 = N.S.	31%	33%	χ^2 = N.S.
Total	(81)	(17)		(29)	(6)	
	100%	100%		100%	100%	

Student's Humanitarianism

	High			Low		
Student Activism	*Mother's Humanitarianism*			*Mother's Humanitarianism*		
	High	Low		High	Low	
Active	(42)	(2)	e = 29%	(10)	(3)	e = −18%
	41%	12%	χ^2 = .05	32%	50%	χ^2 = N.S.
Total	(103)	(17)		(31)	(6)	
	100%	100%		100%	100%	

As a result of this specification under the condition of high student humanitarianism, an important decision emerges: Should the middle-range theory stating mother's humanitarianism led to student humanitarianism, which was associated with student activism, be rejected because the anticipated interpretation of the original relationship did not occur? In this case, as in other similar cases, we decided that this type of specification provided evidence *for* the theory linking mother's humanitarianism with student's humanitarianism and activism, much the same way a finding of interpretation would have provided support for this theory. We will try to establish why the data were analyzed this way.

We examined the literature in survey analysis to find examples where the analyst expected to find interpretation of the original two-variable relationship but instead got specification. Unfortunately, there are very few published examples available in the basic texts on survey analysis, even though Hirschi and Selvin report that the most common result of introducing third variables into a two-variable relationship is specification.[6] However, Rosenberg, in his recent up-dating of Hyman and Lazarsfeld, notes the possibility that specification could provide evidence for a given interpretation of the original relationship.[7]

Rosenberg states as a general principle that "Conditional Relationships May Support or Strengthen the Original Interpretation."[8] He gives as an example the finding that children of divorced families tend to have lower self-esteem than children from intact families. The interpretation of this finding was that children of divorced parents have experienced particularly discordant lives and feel stigmatized by their socially anomalous positions; these experiences, in turn, have a deleterious effect upon their self-esteem.[9] If this interpretation of the original relationship between children of divorced families and self-esteem were correct, Rosenberg argues, the original relationship should be more pronounced among groups where divorce is most socially condemned. This is so because the social stigma and parental disharmony in divorced families should be greater and the effect of divorce on self-esteem should be stronger in groups where divorce is most socially condemned. Thus, the original relationship should be stronger among Jews and Catholics than among Protestants, which he found.[10] He says: "If the relationship of parental divorce and self-esteem were the *same* among Catholics and Jews as among Protestants, this would tend to nullify the interpretation. If, on the other hand, the relationship were *stronger* among Catholics and Jews than among Protestants, the result would tend to confirm it."[11] Thus, Rosenberg argues his case for interpretation of the original two-variable relationship *not* on a reduction of the original relationship in each partial table for each religious group, as would usually be the case for interpretation. Instead, he argues his case for interpretation on the basis of a specification of the original relationship (i.e., the original relationship should increase for some religions, not for all religions).

In addition to Rosenberg's principle about specification, Hyman also notes that one type of specification involves the statement about a variable that intervenes between the independent and dependent variables.[12] He calls this a *contingency* for the original relationship. He gives as an example the specification of political interest for the relationship between sex and voting intention. He feels that political interest intervenes between sex and voting intentions; thus, political interest links the independent and dependent variables. However, Hyman proves this interpretative link *not* by showing a reduction in the original relationship between sex and voting intention in each partial table, as is customary for the classical situation of interpretation. Instead, he proves the intervening link of political interest by showing that the original relationship was most accentuated under the condition of no political interest. His tables, which are adapted here, are presented in Tables 8-3 and 8-4. Thus, Hyman used specification to inter-

Table 8-3
The Relationship Between Sex and Intention to Vote

	Sex		
Intention to Vote	Men	Women	
Yes	98%	82%	e = 16%
No	2%	18%	
Total	100%	100%	

Source: Adapted from Herbert Hyman, *Survey Design and Analysis,* Copyright 1955 by The Free Press, Table XXVI, p. 297.

pret the original relationship—that is, he proved that political interest was the intervening link between sex and intention to vote by showing that sex has most influence on voting intentions under the condition of no political interest.

This is the same type of reasoning we would use for the argument concerning the relationship between mother's humanitarianism, student's humanitarianism, and activism. The relationship between mother's humanitarianism and activism becomes accentuated under the condition of high student humanitarianism. But this would serve to verify the notion that there are links between mother's humanitarianism, student's humanitarianism, and activism. This is so because it is primarily those students adequately socialized to a humanitarian viewpoint (i.e., those high on humanitarianism) who would be expected by this theory to engage in activism. Thus, the specification of the original relationship for students high on humanitarianism is taken by us as evidence for this particular middle-range theory linking mother's humanitarianism to student's humanitarianism and activism.

Romanticism

There is virtually no evidence linking parental romanticism to student romanticism and activism. Almost no original relationship exists between father's romanticism and student activism (e = 3 percent). This increases slightly to e = 11 percent under a condition of *low* student romanticism but reverses slightly to e = −1 percent under a condition of high student romanticism. Thus, by either test of interpretation the predicted statistical relations do not occur when the third variable of student romanticism is introduced. That is, the partial relationships do not all decrease when the

Table 8-4
The Relationship Between Sex and Intention to Vote, with Level of Political Interest Controlled

Level of Political Interest

Intention to Vote	Great			Moderate			None		
	Sex			*Sex*			*Sex*		
	Men	*Women*		*Men*	*Women*		*Men*	*Women*	
Yes	99%	98%	e = 1%	98%	87%	e = 11%	83%	44%	e = 39%
No	1%	2%		2%	13%		17%	56%	
Total	100%	100%		100%	100%		100%	100%	

Source: Adapted from Herbert Hyman, *Survey Design and Analysis*, Copyright 1955 by The Free Press, Table XXVII, p. 297.

third variable is introduced; and the partial table of high romanticism does not show an increase in the original relationship. Furthermore, there is an initial inverse relationship between mother's romanticism and activism (e = −6 percent). This reverses to a very slight positive relationship under a condition of low student romanticism (e = 2 percent), and increases to an even more negative relationship under a condition of high student romanticism (e = −10 percent). So if anything, there is evidence for a slight negative relationship between mother's romanticism, student's romanticism, and activism. Clearly there is no evidence here supporting the view of positive links between these variables.

Intellectualism and Cooperative Values

Another non-conventional value that activists are said to learn at home is intellectualism. However, the 1968 Berkeley data do not lend strong support to this thesis. There is no original relationship between father's intellectualism and activism (e = 2 percent). This is not changed under conditions of either high or low student intellectualism when this third variable is introduced into the original relationship. However, there is a positive relationship between mother's intellectualism and activism of e = 15 percent, but this is essentially unchanged when student intellectualism is introduced as a third variable to test for interpretation. For the interpretation thesis that mother's intellectualism leads to student's intellectualism, which is associated with activism to get substantiation, it would be necessary for the original relation of e = 15 percent to decrease under conditions of high and low student intellectualism, or to increase under a condition of high student intellectualism. Neither occurred when the third variable was introduced. Thus, there seems to be an association between mother's intellectualism and activism, but other factors than student's intellectualism seem to be at work in interpreting the original relationship. We even speculated that the general cultural milieu in intellectual families that sensitizes students to issues of social concern might later be translated into activism. However, this was not borne out. Thus, similar to the case of romanticism, our data do not indicate the direct links between parental intellectualism, student intellectualism, and activism suggested by the cultural approach to activism.

Another measure of intellectual orientation among activists is their presumed high grade point average (GPA). However there are various studies which challenge this assumption.[13] Also, our own data do not lend support to the proposition that most activists have unusually high GPAs. When grade point average is taken as the independent variable, there is almost no association between GPA and activism (dyx = .039).

There has been some speculation recently that the earlier findings of a positive relation between GPA and activism could have been spurious because many graduate students were activists and graduate students almost always have a "B" average or better (3.00 on a 4.00 grade point scale).[14] Thus, our sample was broken into graduate and undergraduate students to test this recent speculation. We found that undergraduate activists tended to be concentrated at the moderate level of grade point average. However, only about 16 percent of the undergraduate activists had low grade point averages. The graduate student activists, as the speculation has it, were concentrated heavily among those with a high grade point average, and literally no graduate student activist had a low GPA. The apparent accuracy of this type of speculation about GPA and activism could indicate some spuriousness for the earlier finding of a general positive relation between GPA and activism.

In sum, there are varied findings with regard to GPA and student activism:

1. There is little overall relation between GPA and activism.
2. Graduate students do tend to confirm the stereotype of excellence in scholarship among activists.
3. Undergraduate activists are more average in their GPA accomplishments.
4. Few activists—undergraduates or graduates—are really poor students.

When these findings on GPA and activism are combined with the other data discussed, we must conclude that there is not much evidence for intellectualism as a general condition of student activism, but this is especially the case for undergraduate activists.

Similarly, there is not much evidence in our data for the predicted links between cooperative values of the parents, cooperative values of the students, and activism. There is an initial positive relation between both father's and mother's cooperative values and activism (e's of 16 percent and 8 percent, respectively). However, when student's cooperative values is introduced as the third test variable, the expected interpretations do not occur for fathers or mothers. Again, the direct links between cooperative parental values, cooperative student values, and activism are not in evidence.

Expressivity of Impulses

It is said that activists do not feel the usual constraints over expressing impulses, such as sexual gratification, and that they learned this more relaxed morality at home. As with the other unconventional values, we would expect an interpretation of the original relationship between parental views on expressing impulses and activism, but this does not happen in our data. The original relationship for father's expressivity of impulses and activism is e = 15 percent. This *decreases* to c = 6 percent under the condition of high student expressivity of impulses and *increases* under the condition of low student expressivity of impulses to a substantial e = 46 percent. (There are only a few cases here, but the relationship of e = 46 percent is statistically significant at the .01 level by the Chi-Square test.) For mothers the same thing happens: the original relationship of e = 17 percent decreases to e = 11 percent when students are high on expressivity of impulses and increases to e = 24 percent when students are low on expressivity of impulses. Hence, interpretation by the conventional method or by the method of specifying contingent relationships is not indicated for fathers or mothers. It is difficult to know why these reversals from predictions occur. Perhaps the relationship between expressivity of impulses and activism is a good deal more complex than previously understood.

In sum the only unconventional, non-political value that operates as the cultural theory would predict is mother's humanitarianism. This is not to say that no positive two-variable relationships exist between activism and the other values of romanticism, intellectualism, cooperation, or expressivity of impulses. On the contrary, our data do indicate that at least some two-variable relationships exist between these parental values and activism (e.g., a positive relationship of e = 15 percent exists between fathers' expressivity of impulses and activism). But the virtue of the method of systematically introducing third test variables is to examine whether or not the original two-variable relationships operate as the theorist thinks they do. We have shown that only for mother's humanitarianism are there the predicted links between parent's unconventional cultural values, student's unconventional cultural values, and student activism. These links do not seem to exist in the same way for father's humanitarianism, and parent's cooperation, romanticism, intellectualism, or expressivity of impulses.

Although the predicted links do not generally exist between these cultural variables, the existence of some positive two-variable relations suggests that culturally distinct families are somehow implicated in activism.[15] Instead of specific values like student's romanticism linking parental romanticism and activism, we expected, for example, that humanitarianism in the cultural milieu of these families might be associated with activism; but when we empirically examined this speculation, it received no support. Thus, more explicitly political values were examined to see whether they might intervene between these culturally distinct family values and activism.

Unconventional Cultural Values, Political Consciousness, and Activism

Drawing on ideas of Flacks and Keniston, we felt that the *liberal* political ideology of the student might intervene between the unconventional cultural values of the parents and activism—that is, liberal political ideology might arise in culturally unconventional families and this liberal political ideology would be translated into activism. Liberal political ideology of the student would thus intervene between the cultural values of the parents and activism rather than the more obvious linking mechanism of the student's cultural values. However, on empirical testing, this speculation did not receive any confirmation whatsoever.

Even though liberal ideology of the student does not seem to intervene between unconventional cultural values of the parents and student activism, quite different results occur when we examine the student's *radical political consciousness*. Our data indicate that student's radical political consciousness does intervene between unconventional cultural values of the parents and student activism. There is moderate to strong support for the following relations:

1. The relationship between parents' intellectualism, student's radical political consciousness, and activism.
2. The relationship between father's cooperative values, student's radical political consciousness, and activism (however, no similar relationship exists for mothers).
3. Parents' expressivity of impulses, student's radical political consciousness, and activism.
4. The relationship between father's humanitarianism, student's radical political consciousness, and activism (however, no similar relationship exists for mothers).[16]

The previous set of findings, taken together, indicate that radical political consciousness and student activism can develop in homes characterized by culturally non-conventional, albeit non-political, values. If radical political consciousness of the parents is one avenue to radical political consciousness and activism of the students, then these culturally unconventional values of the parents amount to another avenue to a student's radical political consciousness and activism. Thus, it appears that students brought up in homes characterized by such values as intellectualism, cooperation, expressivity of impulses, and humanitarianism are about as likely to develop radical political consciousness and become activists as those students brought up in politically radical homes. Undoubtedly, various families that are radically conscious are also characterized by some of these unconventional cultural values. But even when families are not politically radical, it is still possible for students to develop radical views and engage in activism on the basis of the parents' culturally unconventional values.

There is one important distinction to be made in arguing for the derivation of radical consciousness and activism from culturally unconventional homes. There are some cases in which radical political consciousness is a more or less direct outcome of socialization in a family emphasizing culturally distinct values—that is, learning culturally distinct values such as humanitarianism leads to a radical political perspective. However, there is a less direct way that culturally distinctive values of the parents can influence the development of radical political consciousness of the student. This would be the situation where a student was exposed to these cultural values at home, but he did not get exposed to radical political values by his parents. However, these cultural values could be seen as predisposing conditions that would lead the student to adopt a radical political perspective under conditions of stress (to be discussed below) or via another socialization mechanism such as the university he attended.[17] All of these ways that parents' cultural values, student's radical political consciousness, and activism are linked would be consistent with the findings just reported. Our data do not provide an easy way to tell which is the strongest mechanism linking the variables. Nevertheless, there appears to be good evidence supporting the relationship between parents' unconventional cultural values, student's radical political consciousness, and student activism.

As a sort of "final test" of the relative importance of a student's political versus cultural values in generating activism we tried to see how much more of the variation in activism could be explained by a student's cultural values after his political values were taken into account. With few exceptions, the cultural values were not able to explain much more of the variation in activism after a student's radical political consciousness was taken into account.[18] Only the student's attitudes toward drugs and the student's attitudes toward "hippies" were able to explain more of the variation in activism after the student's radical political consciousness was part of the analysis. The other cultural values of students discussed were not able to explain more of the variation in activism; these include student's humanitarianism, expressivity of impulses, cooperation, intellectualism, and romanticism. Even about one-third of the activists were distinctly unfavorable to "hippies," who tend to embody many of these cultural values. So we have a situation in which the *parents'* unconventional cultural values influence activism by generating radical political consciousness in the students; but the *student's* own attachment to unconventional cultural values is not a prime motivator of activism. Thus, the approach stressing cultural alienation of activists receives much less support in our study than the approach focusing on a student's radical political consciousness.

Interpretation of Findings

It is perhaps not surprising that an extreme cultural approach to activism is weak. In a real sense, it is "too unpolitical" an approach to adequately analyze the dynamics of activism. Stated differently, the students who are attached *only* to distinct cultural values often have other outlets for their views than radical politics. For example, those who wish to express impulses can find activities such as "Woodstock." Those interested in humanitarian pursuits can find reformist or non-political causes to associate with instead of non-institutionalized political activism. Similarly, the demands of school work can occupy the interests of students who are intellectually inclined. And the romantics can involve themselves in artistic endeavors. There is no reason why students attached to these unconventional cultural values must participate in anti-Establishment politics.

In fact, for some students attachment to these cultural values can *substitute* for more political commitments. The emphasis among some middle-class students on "changing one's head" can have a distinctly non-political flavor to it. The focus can be quite internal in that the goal of change stops with personality changes for the individual instead of social changes. For example, various middle-class students have complained about cultural and sexual repressiveness in the larger society. But the extent of changes envisioned might only be to search for personal liberation with regard to sexual "hang-ups." Also some who are disenchanted with the rationality of modern life feel that personal experimentation with drugs and religion is sufficient change. There is even a certain type of "false consciousness" that can develop by overattachment to these cultural values—that is, instead of following Mills' dictum to link personal problems with public issues, the emphasis is on solving personal problems quite independent of political and social processes.

Still, we must ask why *parents'* cultural values can have political consequences for students? Especially under conditions of stress, cultural values of the parents get translated politically for students. Conditions of stress can force students to see political implications of parental values that are distinct from conventional Protestant Ethic values. Here, we first examine how the unconventional cultural values are distinct from Protestant Ethic values and then we examine the political consequences of these cultural values.

The Protestant Ethic is a composite value system made up of such specific values as individualism, social mobility, hard work, and delayed gratification. Max Weber felt these values were an inherent part of Western Protestantism and that they influenced the development of rational bourgeois capitalism. Although the American value system is complex, one set of standards usually included in characterizing American values is the Protestant Ethic. Hence any values that are opposite of Protestant Ethic values would be considered unconventional values.

Expressivity of impulses could be looked at as the opposite of the delayed gratification required for the value of social mobility. If an individual wants to improve his position socially and economically, it is often required that he suppress many of his impulses at least temporarily instead of expressing them at will. Expressivity of impulses is often more a characteristic of "hippies" who have rejected mobility values and have opted for more immediate gratification of impulses.

Similarly, the value of cooperation could be seen as the opposite of the Protestant Ethic value of individualism. The value of cooperation emphasizes the collective good rather than the individual good. The value of cooperation sees various individuals combining for the common welfare instead of a given individual attempting to maximize his benefits to the detriment of others, if necessary. The operational definition of the concept of cooperation used here emphasizes its unconventional aspects. As Appendix C indicates, cooperation is operationally defined in terms of antagonism to competitive values. Competition, of course, is usually included as a basic American value.

In a similar fashion, humanitarianism could be seen as the opposite of individualism. The larger entity of "humanity" (or the common welfare) is the focus of concern, not any given individual. As with cooperation, humanitarianism is operationally defined to emphasize its unconventional aspects—that is, stressing the importance to a child of being aware of and concerned about social injustice. It is likely that only a minority of American families strongly emphasize concern about social injustice to their children.

Finally, intellectualism could be viewed as the opposite of the tendency to accept existing social arrangements. The Protestant Ethic has been used to justify existing social arrangements by stating that those who are presently privileged deserve the privileges because they work harder than others. Intellectualism can involve a critical appraisal of existing social arrangements, not just an acceptance of them. Actually, one way intellectualism can challenge the *status quo* is by criticizing such notions that material privileges only come from hard work.

In attempting to understand how these unconventional cultural values of the parents get translated politically for activist students, it is important to remember that Protestant Ethic values underlie the social system of mid-twentieth century America. Being brought up in homes where parents espouse values antagonistic to Protestant Ethic values thus generates the *potential* for students to call into question the larger social system. Undoubtedly, there are students who routinely see political implications of their parents' unconventional cultural values. For example, there are students who feel that a social system that stresses mobility and individual competition will produce inequalities. Hence, a political opposition to that social system would promote equality. However, it is particularly under conditions of *stress* that we would expect these cultural values to get translated into radical consciousness and student activism. Concretely, the various stresses associated with the Vietnam War and the various failures to produce broad social change during the 1960s can be seen as conditions that led to the radicalization of students from culturally unconventional family backgrounds. The cultural values would be predisposing conditions that could be activated politically under conditions of stress. But it is necessary for the parents' cultural values to actually get translated into radical consciousness for the student to be likely to engage in activism. Without the development of radical political consciousness, a given student is not likely to engage in activism solely on the basis of the cultural values. Yet under conditions of stress, there are clear pressures for radical consciousness and activism to develop for students socialized in these culturally unconventional families.[19]

Thus, when we examine both the unconventional cultural values and the unconventional political values that characterize the families of various activists, we can conclude that many activists do come from distinctive ideological backgrounds. The value systems of the families of activists are different from and in many ways opposite of more usual American political and cultural values. In at least some important respects the parents of the activists, as well as the activists themselves, have questioned the values of the existing "Establishment." This conclusion is in keeping with the thrust of arguments developed by such commentators as Flacks and Keniston, but the relations between the specific variables have been shown to be more complex than is usually discussed. Finally, although the political and cultural family backgrounds of activists are distinctive, Chapter 9 indicates that the social-economic backgrounds of activists are not as unusual.

Social Alienation and Activism

There is yet another theory of student activism that focuses on alienation. This is not cultural alienation as we have been discussing it, but social alienation. According to this approach students are socially alienated, and this alienation leads to participation in instances of activism as well as to the development of radical ideology. This is the "mass society theory" applied to the analysis of student activism. [20] There are various ways to empirically test this approach to activism; but only one test of the theory receives support in our data.

The one aspect of mass society theory that receives support involves the fact that activists who are socially alienated in an objective sense (e.g., students who live in an apartment alone) are more likely than others to engage in activism. However, students who are alienated in a subjective sense (e.g., students who feel lonely) are not at all more likely to engage in activism than others. In fact, activists are a bit more likely to disagree than agree that students at U.C. Berkeley are unfriendly. In sum, there is mixed evidence when we examine two-variable relations between social alienation and activism.

A more sophisticated test of the mass society theory of activism examines three-variable relationships. Mass society theory not only states a two-variable relationship between social alienation and activism; it also states that the relationship between the ideology of the students and student activism can be "explained away." The approach argues that the only reason a statistical relationship exists between ideology and activism is because of their common association with a third variable, social alienation. Isolated students or those who feel lonely on campus would, by this theory, be expected to be radically conscious and activist; but the relationship would be spurious.

When student's residence is introduced as a third test variable, there is virtually no change in the original relationship between radical consciousness and activism. For the argument about spuriousness between radical consciousness and activism to be acceptable, it would have been necessary for the statistical association between radical consciousness and activism to become reduced in all partial tables, which did not occur. When the subjective measure of social alienation is introduced as a third variable to similarly test for spuriousness, the anticipated reduction in all partial tables does not occur. There is some specification of the original relationship (the original relationship between radical consciousness and activism slightly increases under the condition of low subjective alienation). But the original relationship is certainly not explained away. Thus, a "mass society theory" attempting to explain away the original relationship between radical political consciousness and student activism does not receive confirmation in these data.

Conclusion

In this chapter we have attempted to gather data on approaches to activism that stress cultural and social alienation. In general, not much support for these approaches was found. They are both "too unpolitical" to explain the dynamics of activism. On the other hand, there is support for an approach indicating political consequences of socialization in culturally unconventional families. There is strong evidence in our data that a student's radical political views and participation in activism are influenced by the unconventional cultural values of his or her parents. This type of finding, in turn, lends important support to our own theory of activism—that is, many activists act in terms of radical values derived from their parents' radical political *or* culturally unconventional values, yet come into conflict with their parents over these same values.

Notes

1. See, for example, Richard Flacks, "Social and Cultural Meanings of Student Revolt: Some Informal Comparative Observations," *Social Problems* 17 (Winter 1970): 340-57; Richard Flacks, "The Liberated Generation: An Exploration of the Roots of Student Protest," *The Journal of Social Issues* 23 (July 1967): 52-75; Kenneth Keniston, *Youth and Dissent* (New York: Harcourt Brace Jovanovich, 1971); Kenneth Keniston, *Young Radicals* (New York: Harcourt, Brace & World, 1968).

2. Theodore Roszak, *The Making of a Counter Culture* (Garden City, N.Y.: Anchor Books, 1969).

3. Ibid., pp. 56-83.

4. See, for example, Seymour Martin Lipset, *Rebellion in the University* (Boston: Little, Brown & Co., 1972), p. 104.

5. We have relied on Flacks' general definitions for some of these concepts. See Flacks, "The Liberated Generation," op. cit., pp. 69-70. However we have supplied our own operational definitions of the concepts; see Appendix C.

6. Travis Hirschi and Hanan C. Selvin, *Delinquency Research: An Appraisal of Analytic Methods* (New York: The Free Press, 1971), p. 47.

7. Morris Rosenberg, *The Logic of Survey Analysis* (New York: Basic Books, 1968), pp. 109-12, 236-37.

8. Ibid., pp. 109-12.

9. Ibid., p. 236.

10. Ibid.

11. Ibid.

12. Herbert Hyman, *Survey Design and Analysis,* Copyright 1955 by The Free Press, pp. 305-7.

13. Lipset summarizes various studies that challenge the presumed positive relationship between GPA and activism. See Lipset, op. cit., pp. 108-9; and Seymour Martin Lipset and Philip G. Altbach, "Student Politics and Higher Education in the United States," *Comparative Education Review* 10 (June 1966): 333-4.

14. Two recent critics of the older finding of activists having high grade point averages are Travis Hirschi and Joseph Zelan. See their as yet unpublished papers: Travis Hirschi and Joseph Zelan, "Student Activism: A Critical Review of the Literature and Preliminary Analysis of the Carnegie Commission Data on Graduate Students"; and Joseph Zelan, "Undergraduate Student Activism," July 1971. Both Hirschi and Zelan were associated with the Survey Research Center at the University of California, Berkeley when they wrote these papers.

15. In addition to the way discussed in the body of this chapter, we discovered *ex post facto* that parents' unconventional cultural values could compensate for the student being low on the value of humanitarianism in producing participation in activism. For example, the relationship between father's cooperative values and activism increased from an original relationship of e = 20 percent to e = 38 percent under the condition of low student humanitarianism; the parallel increase for mothers was from an original relationship of e = 8 percent to e = 19 percent. We also discovered *ex post facto* that parents' political values—radical or liberal—could compensate for a student being low on various unconventional cultural values in producing participation in activism. For example, the association between mother's radical consciousness and activism increased from an original relation of e = 16 percent to e = 28 percent when the student was low on cooperative values.

16. The links between the cultural values of the parents, student's radical political consciousness, and student activism are empirically demonstrated by the method of "interpretation by specification" discussed in this chapter. The relationship between the cultural values of the parents and activism increases under the condition of high radical political consciousness of the student when student's radical consciousness is introduced as a third variable.

17. In Chapter 6, our data indicated that university socialization occurred for at least a minority of students in our sample.

18. The methodology used to reach these conclusions will be discussed in Chapter 12. It focuses on additive relations between variables—that is, the cultural values of the student were not able to add much to the explanation of activism after the student's radical political consciousness was taken into account.

19. To add one more complexity to our analysis, it should be noted that

these unconventional cultural values are not entirely consistent, yet they seem to have a similar effect on the student's radical consciousness and participation in activism (the only value that did not act similarly was romanticism). For example, if intellectualism emphasizes the more rational aspects of people, then expressivity of impulses emphasizes the more emotional aspects. In addition, expressing one's impulses is part of an individual orientation whereas humanitarianism and cooperation are part of a collective orientation. Of course, there are many individuals who are high on intellectualism, expressivity of impulses, cooperation, and humanitarianism. But there are some distinctions between these four unconventional cultural values. Perhaps the existence of these distinctions makes the similarity of their political consequences even more impressive. In the last chapter we discuss further the role of strain in student activism.

20. For a discussion of the role of social alienation in student activism, see Seymour Martin Lipset, "University Student Politics," in Seymour Martin Lipset and Sheldon S. Wolin, eds., *The Berkeley Student Revolt* (Garden City, N.Y.: Anchor Books, 1965), pp. 5-6.

9

The Social-Economic
Background of Activists

Introduction

Many commentators have remarked about the distinctive—and often favored—social-economic background of activists. It has been said that activists tend to be overrepresented among upper status families, professional families, Jewish families, highly educated families, families with an urban background, affluent families, and families in which mothers were very well educated and involved in their own careers.[1] The position that American activists are from generally favored backgrounds is parallel to the view that in other countries middle- and upper-class youth have participated in various rebellions and revolutions. However, there are other discussions that point to a broadening social-economic base of the student movement by the latter part of the Sixties. Instead of the movement being comprised of those from distinctive backgrounds, other groups were seen to become increasingly involved in the political protests. The other groups included Roman Catholics and Protestants, the offspring of businessmen, white-collar and blue-collar workers, and youth raised as Republicans in "middle America."[2]

Our data permit an examination of the proposition that the student movement had changed its "base" by the late 1960s. In particular, we can examine the social-economic background of students who participated in political protests in the years of 1964, 1966, and 1967. The reader will recall that our general index of student activism is made up of the following instances of student protest: (1) the Free Speech Movement of 1964; (2) the Student Strike at U.C. Berkeley in 1966; and (3) the Oakland Induction Center demonstration in 1967. If we "decompose" this index into its three separate components, we can see whether the social background of student activists changed over time.

Our data indicate a picture more complex than either of the above views on the social background of activists. On one hand, there is only a weak overall relationship between social-economic background and activism. Similarly, there is some evidence of a broadening base of the movement. Still, where differences exist between activists, they tend to be the differences predicted by the approach stressing the distinctive backgrounds of activists. Finally, we also find evidence for a curvilinear relationship between social background and activism. Thus, in contrast to our positive findings about the distinctive political and cultural backgrounds of activists, we see a more complicated set of findings for the social-economic background of activists. This means that in our study, many activists were socialized in families with distinctive political and cultural views, but these views characterized families from varying social-economic levels.

The Findings

Conclusions about the social-economic base of the movement and any changes it might have undergone over time can be drawn from Tables 9-1 and 9-2 which should be examined together.[3] Table 9-1 gives the proportion of student activists for various groups of students for each of the three instances of activism in our study (e.g., Table 9-1 gives the proportion of Protestants who participated in the Free Speech Movement; the proportion of students whose fathers were professionals and who participated in the Student Strike of 1966; and the proportion of students whose fathers were Conservative Republicans and who participated in the Oakland Induction Center demonstration of 1967). Table 9-2 shows the percentage differences between various groups of student activists over time. For example, it shows whether Jewish students were more likely than Protestants to be activists in 1964 as compared to 1966 or 1967; also it shows whether students whose fathers were professionals were more likely than students whose fathers were managers to be activists in 1964 as compared to 1966 or 1967.

According to the hypothesis of a broadening base of the movement, there should be a decreasing percentage difference between the various groups of activists over time. If there were an actual changing base of the movement by 1967, we would expect a decreasing percentage difference in proportion activists over time (1) between Jews, Protestants, and Catholics; (2) between students whose fathers were Liberal Democrats versus more conservative fathers; (3) between students whose families were affluent as opposed to less well-off; (4) between students whose mothers were involved in trained occupations (here the term is "People-Oriented" occupations) and students whose mothers were in other occupations or who were housewives; (5) between students whose mothers were Democrats versus more conservative mothers; (6) between students whose fathers were very well educated versus students whose fathers were less well educated; and (7) between students whose mothers were very well educated versus students whose mothers were less well educated.

As Table 9-2 shows, only a few of the relationships indicate the predicted steady decrease over time. Other differences increase over time, and there are curvillinear relationships in these data. There is, for example, evidence of a decreasing percentage difference between activists whose mothers are in Sales. From 1964 to 1966 to 1967 there is a steady decrease in percentage difference of activists between these two groups of e = 42 percent, e = 23 percent, and e = 3 percent. But there are really only a few other cases of this steady decrease that would be predicted by the hypothesis concerning a broadening base of the movement.

A somewhat more arguable case for the Berkeley campus could be made for the assertion that group differences for activists were initially small during the Free Speech Movement, increased over time by 1966, but again became less apparent by 1967. This would be an argument for a curvilinear relationship. For example, there was almost no greater likelihood that FSM activists would come from a family where the father was a professional rather than a manager. However, the activists in the 1966 student strike were more likely to have a professional than managerial father; but the activists at the 1967 demonstration at the Oakland Induction Center were similar to the FSM activists in that they were not more likely to come from families with professional versus managerial fathers. This type of curvilinear relationship also holds for: (1) Jewish versus Protestant students; (2) students whose fathers are Liberal Democrats versus Liberal Republicans, as well as Liberal Democrats versus Conservative Democrats; (3) students whose mothers are Democrats versus Republicans; and (4) students whose fathers have Ph.D. degrees versus students whose fathers have less than high school education, as well as fathers who graduated from high school, those who graduated from college, and those who have Master's degrees.

We should point out that the preceding data showing small differences between groups by 1967 do lend support to the thesis of a broadening base of the student movement. These data—even when part of a curvilinear relationship—show that in the latter part of the 1960s there were people from various groups participating in student activism. And to these data should be added data on family income. Although there are several reversals in the table, still by 1967 there were only small differences in proportion activists between the affluent and the less affluent.

Of course, the data in Table 9-2 also indicate large differences between other groups by 1967. The data should be taken to reject the thesis of the broadening base of the movement for these groups. Some of the groups that reject the thesis are: (1) Jewish versus Catholic students; (2) students whose fathers are professionals versus clerks, skilled laborers, and farmers; (3) students whose mothers are in People-Oriented occupations versus administration, skilled labor, clerical work, or who are housewives; (4) students whose fathers have Ph.D. degrees versus students whose fathers have some graduate school or a law degree; and (5) students whose mothers have a Master's degree versus students whose mothers are at all

Table 9-1
The Social-Economic Background of Student Activists Over Time

Social-Economic Background Characteristics of Student Activists	Year and Instance of Student Activism		
	1964 (FSM)	1966 (Student Strike)	1967 (Oakland Induction Center)
1. Student's Religion			
Protestant	34% (62)	21% (136)	17% (216)
Catholic	28% (29)	25% (48)	11% (70)
Jewish	45% (20)	43% (42)	32% (63)
2. Father's Occupation			
Manager	38% (47)	21% (80)	18% (130)
Professional	42% (48)	34% (94)	21% (152)
Clerk	43% (7)	19% (21)	9% (32)
Skilled Labor	40% (10)	28% (25)	7% (43)
Farmer	0% (3)	0% (7)	0% (7)
Other	25% (12)	25% (28)	28% (39)
3. Father's Political Party			
Conservative Republican	18% (27)	12% (52)	14% (89)
Liberal Republican	53% (17)	26% (43)	21% (71)
Conservative Democrat	36% (42)	19% (73)	13% (106)
Liberal Democrat	43% (30)	44% (59)	25% (92)
Democratic Socialist	75% (4)	56% (9)	36% (14)
Revolutionary Socialist	0% (0)	0% (1)	0% (2)
Other	27% (11)	31% (26)	16% (38)
4. Family Income			
$5,000 and under	25% (8)	36% (14)	15% (26)
$5,001-9,999	24% (21)	24% (46)	13% (70)
$10,000-14,999	39% (31)	28% (61)	18% (92)
$15,000-24,999	46% (28)	33% (54)	24% (92)
$25,000 and over	35% (20)	16% (43)	21% (62)
5. Mother's Occupation[a]			
People-Oriented	75% (8)	38% (16)	30% (23)
Arts	0% (0)	100% (2)	67% (3)

Professional	0% (0)	0% (2)	0% (4)
Sales	33% (6)	15% (13)	27% (15)
Administration	0% (1)	0% (1)	0% (2)
Skilled Labor	0% (1)	0% (1)	0% (1)
Unskilled Labor	0% (1)	0% (1)	20% (5)
Clerical	38% (8)	23% (13)	19% (31)
Other Occupations	0% (1)	100% (1)	0% (0)
Housewife	32% (25)	37% (54)	20% (94)
6. Mother's Political Party			
Right-Wing	0% (0)	50% (2)	50% (2)
Republican	31% (16)	18% (40)	15% (78)
Democrat	37% (30)	43% (54)	24% (85)
Socialist	100% (1)	0% (1)	100% (1)
7. Father's Education			
Less than High School	35% (20)	20% (41)	11% (62)
High School Graduate	26% (27)	27% (12)	16% (71)
Some College	54% (22)	24% (45)	25% (81)
College Graduate	32% (28)	19% (57)	19% (85)
Some Graduate School	25% (4)	27% (11)	6% (17)
Law Degree	60% (5)	29% (14)	10% (20)
Master's Degree	38% (13)	35% (23)	26% (38)
Ph. D. Degree	33% (12)	44% (25)	22% (37)
8. Mother's Education			
Less than High School	23% (13)	21% (33)	7% (45)
High School Graduate	36% (42)	23% (78)	16% (127)
Some College	37% (27)	27% (62)	17% (106)
College Graduate	31% (29)	21% (53)	21% (82)
Some Graduate School	67% (6)	46% (13)	22% (18)
Law Degree	0% (0)	0% (0)	0% (0)
Master's Degree	64% (11)	44% (18)	42% (26)
Ph. D. Degree	0% (2)	50% (4)	33% (6)

Note: The numbers in parentheses represent the total number on which the percentage is based (e.g., in the 1964 FSM data, 34 percent of 62 Protestants are student activists).

[a]The coding schema for Mother's Occupation distinguishes between "People-Oriented" occupations and Professionals and Arts. However, People-Oriented occupations would include professions such as teaching, social work, and nursing. The few non-People-Oriented professionals would possibly include isolated chemists and physicists. Possibly artists were felt to be isolated too.

Table 9-2
Comparison of Percentage Differences Over Time Between Categories of Student Activists

Social-Economic Background Comparisons of Student Activists	Year and Instance of Student Activism		
	1964 (FSM)	1966 (Student Strike)	1967 (Oakland Induction Center)
1. Student's Religion			
Jewish vs. Protestant	11%	22%	15%
Jewish vs. Catholic	17%	18%	21%
2. Father's Occupation			
Professional vs. Manager	4%	13%	3%
Professional vs. Clerk	-1%	15%	12%
Professional vs. Skilled Labor	2%	6%	14%
Professional vs. Farmer	42%	34%	21%
3. Father's Political Party			
Liberal Democrat vs. Conservative Republican	25%	32%	11%
Liberal Democrat vs. Liberal Republican	-10%	18%	4%
Liberal Democrat vs. Conservative Democrat	7%	25%	12%
Liberal Democrat vs. Democratic Socialist	-32%	-12%	-11%
Liberal Democrat vs. Revolutionary Socialist	43%	44%	25%
Liberal Democrat vs. Other	16%	13%	9%
4. Family Income			
$25,000 and Over vs. $5,000 and Under	10%	-20%	6%
$25,000 and Over vs. $5,001-9,999	11%	-8%	8%
$25,000 and Over vs. $10,000-14,999	-4%	-12%	3%
$25,000 and Over vs. $15,000-24,999	-11%	-17%	-3%

5. Mother's Occupation

People-Oriented vs. Arts	75%	-62%	-37%
People-Oriented vs. Professional	75%	38%	30%
People-Oriented vs. Sales	42%	23%	3%
People-Oriented vs. Administration	75%	38%	30%
People-Oriented vs. Skilled Labor	75%	38%	30%
People-Oriented vs. Unskilled Labor	75%	38%	10%
People-Oriented vs. Clerical	37%	15%	11%
People-Oriented vs. Other Occupation	75%	-62%	30%
People-Oriented vs. Housewife	43%	1%	10%

6. Mother's Political Party

Democrat vs. Right Wing	37%	-7%	-26%
Democrat vs. Republican	6%	25%	9%
Democrat vs. Socialist	-63%	43%	-76%

7. Father's Education

Ph. D. degree vs. Less than High School	-2%	24%	11%
Ph. D. degree vs. High School graduate	7%	17%	6%
Ph. D. degree vs. some College	-21%	20%	-3%
Ph. D. degree vs. College graduate	1%	25%	3%
Ph. D. degree vs. some Graduate School	8%	17%	16%
Ph. D. degree vs. Law degree	-27%	15%	12%
Ph. D. degree vs. Master's degree	-5%	9%	-4%

8. Mother's Education

Master's degree vs. Less than High School	41%	23%	35%
Master's degree vs. High School graduate	28%	21%	26%
Master's degree vs. some College	27%	17%	25%
Master's degree vs. College graduate	33%	23%	21%
Master's degree vs. some Graduate School	-3%	-2%	20%
Master's degree vs. Law degree	64%	44%	42%
Master's degree vs. Ph. D. degree	64%	-6%	9%

Note: For the data from which these percentage differences were derived, see Table 9-1. Since some of the original percents were based on only a few cases, the reader is advised to examine Table 9-1 for the number of cases involved for any given comparison.

other educational levels, except perhaps students whose mothers have a Ph.D. degree. Thus, the base of the Berkeley student movement had broadened by the latter part of the 1960s to include greater proportions of some groups. Yet some differences in likelihood of participation in activism did exist by the latter part of the 1960s, and for the most part these were differences related to the presumed distinctiveness of activists' social-economic background.

The Decrease of Activism at Berkeley

An examination of Table 9-1 indicates possibly the most interesting fact of all in the analysis of changes in student activism over time: *for almost all background characteristics, there has been a steady decrease in proportion of activists from the Free Speech Movement in 1964 to 1967.* Thus, from 1964 to 1966 to 1967 there was a steady decrease in proportion of Jewish students who were activists from 45 percent to 43 percent to 32 percent; similarly for Protestant students: 34 percent to 21 percent to 17 percent. The same holds for students whose fathers were professionals: 42 percent of these students were activists in 1964, but only 34 percent were in 1966, and this decreased to 21 percent by 1967. Again, 46 percent of those students whose families earned $15,000 to $24,999 were activists in 1964, but 33 percent were activists in 1966, whereas 24 percent were activists in 1967. Certainly there are reversals in Table 9-1. But the trend toward a lessening proportion of activists in each background category is unmistakable. Even though the proportion of activists was to dramatically increase in every category a few years later because of Cambodia, these data seem to indicate that a decreasing proportion of students were involved in the Berkeley movement over time.

In sum, these data on the background of student activists indicate *both* a partial broadening of the base of the student movement at Berkeley by 1967 *and* a decreasing involvement in student activism by most categories of student—that is, some of the background differences between activists had diminished by 1967 (although others remained or even increased). Yet a smaller proportion of all groups of students were participating in activism by 1967.

The ideas of a broadening base of the movement *and* a decrease in proportion of student involvement in the movement seem somehow incompatible. In a statistical sense, however, they are not incompatible. It is possible for fewer students to be involved in a movement over time, but for the movement to increasingly recruit people from varying backgrounds nevertheless. Our data point to this dual tendency.

The contradictions of the Vietnam War are probably the best explanation of this dual set of findings. At Berkeley, there was an increasingly militant response to the Vietnam War. This militancy appealed to a smaller number of people than the Free Speech Movement. The FSM was much more of a reformist movement, which appealed to broad student interests such as better education and free speech. Probably those who were most committed to militant actions remained in the student movement and those less committed to militant actions dropped out of the movement after FSM. However, the Vietnam War—and the military draft associated with it —negatively affected students from all social-economic backgrounds. Thus, Vietnam could have the dual effect of broadening the base of the Berkeley movement *and* causing a decline in numbers of participants.

By the time of Cambodia, political protests against U.S. involvement in Asia were more or less legitimate. As a result, much of the political activity over Cambodia was reformist in nature and thereby had widespread support. For example, various students tried to discuss the war with people in surrounding neighborhoods, and there were various petition-signing campaigns aimed at legislating an end to U.S. intervention in Asia. Actually, many radical activists had difficulty relating to the political protests over Cambodia because these were so reformist.[4] Thus, even though many students were involved in Cambodian protests, it appears that there was a decline of student participation in the Berkeley New Left as early as 1966 and 1967.[5]

There remains an important question: How can we reconcile the diminishing number of students in the Berkeley student movement by 1967 with the apparent fact that the student movement throughout the country was gaining in numbers by 1967? Skolnick presents a chart showing a steady increase in numbers of anti-war protesters on the national level from 1965 to 1968.[6] Similarly Lipset, using data from the Harris Survey, shows that from 1965 to 1969 to 1970 the proportion of students who were involved in some kind of demonstration increased from 29 percent to 40 percent to 60 percent of the U.S. student population.[7] These are good empirical data —possibly as good as the data indicating decreasing student activism at Berkeley. Thus, it seems that the national protest movement was increasing in numbers throughout the Sixties, but the Berkeley movement was decreasing.

It is likely that the Berkeley movement against the war was more militant than the national anti-war movement. Although the war was negatively affecting more and more people on the national level, many national protests occurred without direct confrontations with the police. Also, the growing national anti-war sentiment did not necessarily imply a radical anti-imperialist ideology by demonstrators. Of course, such anti-imperialist ideology was adhered to by many students throughout the country. But, as noted, anti-war protest became more or less legitimate by the time of the Cambodian protests. Thus the increasing legitimacy of anti-war sentiment and the lower level of militancy were important to the growth of the national movement, but the increasing militancy at Berkeley was probably responsible for a decline in proportion of activists there.

Conclusion

In this chapter, we have seen only a weak general relationship between social-economic background characteristics and student activism. The view that activists come from highly distinctive social-economic backgrounds is not given much support. We have seen evidence for a broadening base of the student movement by the late 1960s. And we have seen evidence of a curvilinear relationship between social-economic background and activism. Although some activists did come from distinctive social-economic backgrounds throughout the 1960s, we cannot say that social-economic background is a generalized source of student activism.

One of the reasons that many commentators felt activists came from distinctive social-economic backgrounds was the impression that these families nurtured particular ideologies in their children. These families were seen as primary carriers of unconventional political and cultural values that they passed on to their activist children. In contrast to this view, our complex data do not permit an inference of consistent links between distinctive social-economic background characteristics, unconventional political or cultural values, and activism. Actually, the only such links we found were between Jewish background, radical political consciousness, and activism.[8] However, even this common stereotype needs qualification: Jewish students had the highest proportionate representation among activists, but there were numerically more Protestant activists (Catholics were lowest in proportion and number of activists among the three main religions at Berkeley).

The absence of links between social-economic background characteristics, political or cultural ideology, and activism does *not* reject our earlier findings about familial sources of activism. In particular, the present findings do not reject our previous findings linking unconventional political or cultural values of parents, radical political consciousness of the student, and activism. It just means that at Berkeley these ideological links between activists and their parents are not confined to families of distinctive social-economic backgrounds.

Notes

1. For example, see Richard Flacks, ''The Liberated Generation: An

Exploration of the Roots of Student Protest," *The Journal of Social Issues* 23 (July 1967): 52-75.

2. For example, see Milton Mankoff and Richard Flacks, "The Changing Social Base of the American Student Movement," *The Annals of The American Academy of Political and Social Science* 395 (May 1971): 60-61. Also see Riley Dunlap, "Radical and Conservative Student Activists: A Comparison of Family Backgrounds," *Pacific Sociological Review* 13 (Summer 1970): 171-81.

3. Tables 9-1 and 9-2 were derived from the students' answers about their own religion, their father's occupation, their father's political party, their family's income, their father's education, and their mother's education; and from the mother's answers about their own occupation and political party since students were not asked these questions. We used the student responses about parental characteristics instead of parental responses in these cases for three reasons: (1) greater comparability to other studies of student activism, which usually use student reports of parental characteristics; (2) the greater number of cases possible when student responses were used; and (3) the fact that there was a generally high association between student and parental reports of these items. However, the association was certainly not perfect on all items, especially in relation to family income. But the larger number of cases with the use of student responses probably makes up for potentially misleading statistics based on fewer cases for parental reports. Also, we are examining comparisons over time in these tables, and if there were some student distortion of parental income, for example, this would likely be similarly distorted from year to year; thus, the relative comparisons would remain valid. A final note on reading the statistics in these and other tables in this book: we have taken out of the samples people who answered " Don't know" or "No answer" to the various items.

4. The reformist nature of the Cambodian protests was, however, briefly preceded by rather high levels of violent confrontation between police and demonstrators. The level of violence is probably why various campus administrators approved, at least tacitly, of reformist politics associated with "restructuring" universities—that is, the political action over Cambodia could be reformist rather than violent when the university was restructured to permit political protests.

5. For an argument that the New Left movement is finished, see Richard Flacks, "The New Left and American Politics After Ten Years," *The Journal of Social Issues* 27, No. 1 (1971): 21-34. In the last chapter of this volume, we discuss the decline of the student movement in more detail.

6. Jerome H. Skolnick, *The Politics of Protest* (New York: Ballantine Books, 1969), Chart II-1, p. 32.

7. Seymour Martin Lipset, *Rebellion in the University* (Boston: Little, Brown & Co., 1972), Table 3, p. 45.

8. Our data indicate that in general Jews are overrepresented among the activists and that their radical political consciousness is an important reason why they are overrepresented among religious groups. Almost half of the Jewish students at Berkeley in 1968 were activists (i.e., almost half of the Jewish students took part in at least one of the three instances of student activism in our index of activism). Approximately one quarter of the Protestants and Catholics, by comparison, were activists in 1968. About a third of students with no religion or those who reported a religion other than Protestant, Catholic, or Jewish were activists. Thus, Jews were proportionately overrepresented among student activists as Flacks, Keniston, Lipset, and others have suggested. Furthermore, when radical political consciousness was held constant, the proportion of activists increased for every religious group under the condition of high radical consciousness. Hence, radical political consciousness would seem to be an intervening link between religion and activism for the group most likely to be activists—i.e., Jewish students.

10 Permissive Childrearing Practices and Activism

Introduction

Commentators from Richard Flacks to Spiro Agnew have argued that activists were brought up in permissive or democratic homes. Although there is some debate over the degree of indulgence in these families, many observers feel that families of activists were relaxed with regard to punishment, strict discipline, and conformity to rules. In addition, activists have been seen as participating in family decisions on a more equal basis than in families of nonactivists. Instead of being told what to do by parents, activists presumably have been permitted from a rather early age to help decide family matters. The teachings of Dr. Benjamin Spock have often been cited as influencing the parents of activists in their childrearing practices. These permissive and democratic childrearing practices have, in turn, been seen as underlying conditions of activism.

It is not always clear why these permissive and democratic childrearing practices should underlie activism. There is often some confusion whether these childrearing practices *give rise* to a student's radical or liberal political ideology, which later gets translated into activism, or whether the childrearing practices *reflect* parental radicalism or liberalism. In the latter formulation, the relationship between childrearing practices and activism could be spurious because both the childrearing practices and student activism would relate independently to a third variable, parental political ideology.

The delineation of the exact way these methods of socialization relate to activism should not detain us long. *Few* links exist between permissive or democratic childrearing practices and student activism, which, of course, is very different from our positive findings about socialization to radical political values in families of activists. The relationship between socialization methods and activism holds mainly for Jewish students; thus, socialization methods by themselves do not seem to be a general source of student activism.

The Findings

An examination of two-variable relationships in Tables 10-1 and 10-2 does

115

Table 10-1
Parents' Democratic Childrearing Practices and Student Activism

Student Activism	Parent	
	Father	
	Democratic Childrearing	
	High	Low
Active	(35)	(15)
	35%	40%
Total	(99)	(37)
	100%	100%

e = −5%
χ² = N.S.

Student Activism	Mother	
	Democratic Childrearing	
	High	Low
Active	(52)	(6)
	40%	19%
Total	(129)	(32)
	100%	100%

e = 21%
χ² = .05

not suggest much association between democratic or permissive childrearing practices and activism. The only evidence that would support this type of relationship concerns mother's democratic socialization practices and activism (see Table 10-1). Evidence on father's democratic socialization practices, as well as on father's and mother's permissive practices (as measured by emphasis on degree of punishment administered in the socialization process) does not lend much support to the hypothesis.

However, further analysis along lines suggested by Lipset partly modifies our conclusion about socialization methods and activism. Lipset feels that there may be some confounding of the two sets of association between religion and activism, and between permissive family background and activism. Reviewing and criticizing prior studies of "left-wing" and "right-wing" student activism, Lipset states:

. . . leftist activists tend to be the offspring of permissive families as judged by childrearing practices, and of families characterized by a strong mother who dominates family life and decisions. Conversely, conservative activists tend to come

Table 10-2

Parents' Permissive Childrearing Practices (Measured by Extent of Punishment) and Student Activism

	Parent		
	Father		
Student Activism	*Childrearing Punishment*		
	High	*Low*	
Active	(13) 30%	(35) 38%	e = −8% χ² = N.S.
Total	(43) 100%	(91) 100%	

	Mother		
Student Activism	*Childrearing Punishment*		
	High	*Low*	
Active	(12) 32%	(44) 36%	e = −4% χ² = N.S.
Total	(37) 100%	(121) 100%	

from families with more strict relationships between parents and children, and in which the father plays a dominant controlling role. But to a considerable extent these differences correspond to little more than the variation reported in studies of Jewish and Protestant families. Childhood rearing practices tend to be linked to socio-cultural-political outlooks. To prove that such factors play an independent role in determining the political choices of students, it will first be necessary to compare students with similar ethnic, religious and political-cultural environments. This has not yet been done.[1]

Thus, if we overlook issues related to conservative activists and Portnoy's Complaint (for which we have no data), Lipset has set for us a problem: Is there an association between religious background, childrearing practices, and student activism? Even though our data do not show strong initial relations between childrearing practices and activism, the introduction of religion as a third test variable does indicate links between religion, childrearing practices, and activism similar to Lipset's predictions.

As Tables 10-3 and 10-4 indicate, the initially weak relations tend to become accentuated for Jews and de-emphasized for Protestants. This is

Table 10-3
Parents' Democratic Childrearing Practices and Student Activism, with Parents' Religion Controlled

Religion

Protestant

Student Activism	Father's Democratic Childrearing		
	High	Low	
Active	(17) 31%	(10) 59%	e = −28% χ² = .05
Total	(55) 100%	(17) 100%	

Catholic

Student Activism	Father's Democratic Childrearing		
	High	Low	
Active	(3) 18%	(4) 31%	e = −13% χ² = N.S.
Total	(17) 100%	(13) 100%	

Jewish

Student Activism	Father's Democratic Childrearing		
	High	Low	
Active	(10) 67%	(1) 17%	e = 50% χ² = .05
Total	(15) 100%	(6) 100%	

Other

Student Activism	Father's Democratic Childrearing		
	High	Low	
Active	(2) 29%	(0) 0%	e = 29% χ² = N.S.
Total	(7) 100%	(0) 100%	

No Answer

	Father's Democratic Childrearing		
	High	Low	
Active	(3) 60%	(0) 0%	e = 60% χ² = N.S.
Total	(5) 100%	(1) 100%	

Religion

Protestant

Student Activism	Mother's Democratic Childrearing High	Low	
Active	(30) 37%	(2) 12%	e = 15%
Total	(82) 100%	(16) 100%	χ² = .10

Catholic

Student Activism	Mother's Democratic Childrearing High	Low	
Active	(5) 31%	(2) 29%	e = 2%
Total	(16) 100%	(7) 100%	χ² = N.S.

Jewish

Student Activism	Mother's Democratic Childrearing High	Low	
Active	(15) 75%	(1) 17%	e = 58%
Total	(20) 100%	(6) 100%	χ² = .02

No Answer

Student Activism	Mother's Democratic Childrearing High	Low	
Active	(1) 33%	(1) 50%	e = −17%
Total	(3) 100%	(2) 100%	χ² = N.S.

Other

Student Activism	Mother's Democratic Childrearing High	Low	
Active	(1) 12%	(0) 0%	e = 12%
Total	(8) 100%	(1) 100%	χ² = N.S.

Table 10-4
Parents' Permissive Childrearing Practices (Measured by Extent of Punishment) and Student Activism, with Parents' Religion Controlled

Religion

Protestant

Student Activism	Father's Childrearing Punishment			
	High	Low		
Active	(5) 23%	(21) 43%	e = −20%	χ² = N.S.
Total	(22) 100%	(49) 100%		

Catholic

Student Activism	Father's Childrearing Punishment			
	High	Low		
Active	(5) 42%	(2) 11%	e = 31%	χ² = .10
Total	(12) 100%	(16) 100%		

Jewish

Student Activism	Father's Childrearing Punishment			
	High	Low		
Active	(1) 20%	(10) 62%	e = −42%	χ² = .10
Total	(5) 100%	(16) 100%		

Other

Student Activism	Father's Childrearing Punishment			
	High	Low		
Active	(2) 67%	(0) 0%	e = 67%	χ² = .10
Total	(3) 100%	(4) 100%		

No Answer

Student Activism	Father's Childrearing Punishment			
	High	Low		
Active	(0) 0%	(2) 50%	e = −50%	χ² = N.S.
Total	(1) 100%	(4) 100%		

Religion

Protestant

Student Activism	Mother's Childrearing Punishment	
	High	Low
Active	(11) 37%	(20) 30%
Total	(30) 100%	(67) 100%

e = 7%
χ^2 = N.S.

Catholic

Student Activism	Mother's Childrearing Punishment	
	High	Low
Active	(0) 0%	(7) 37%
Total	(4) 100%	(19) 100%

e = −37%
χ^2 = N.S.

Jewish

Student Activism	Mother's Childrearing Punishment	
	High	Low
Active	(1) 50%	(15) 62%
Total	(2) 100%	(24) 100%

e = −12%
χ^2 = N.S.

Other

Student Activism	Mother's Childrearing Punishment	
	High	Low
Active	(0) 0%	(0) 0%
Total	(1) 100%	(6) 100%

e = 0%
χ^2 = N.S.

No Answer

Student Activism	Mother's Childrearing Punishment	
	High	Low
Active	(0) 0%	(2) 40%
Total	(0) 100%	(5) 100%

e = −40%
χ^2 = N.S.

not uniformly the case for each comparison in Tables 10-3 and 10-4, but the tendency exists for Jewish activists to come from democratic and permissive families whereas this is less the case for Protestant activists. The other religious categories are mixed and do not exactly relate to Lipset's hypotheses.

Even the Jewish-Protestant comparisons do not relate precisely to Lipset's ideas since we do not have cases of conservative activists such as the Young Americans for Freedom. Also, we have *specified* a religious condition under which certain relations exist whereas Lipset was essentially trying to see if the presumed relationship between permissive childrearing and activism could be "explained away" by religion. Nevertheless, these data do relate to the basic drift of his ideas about comparing Jews and Protestants, and his ideas do receive some support here. In sum, the relation between democratic or permissive childrearing practices and activism is not a generalized relationship; the main group for whom the relation seems to hold is Jewish students. Hence we share Lipset's skepticism about childrearing practices being a general source of student activism.

Notes

1. Seymour Martin Lipset, "The Activists: A Profile," *The Public Interest* Number 13 (Fall 1968): 49-50. Copyright © by National Affairs, Inc., 1968.

11 Reformist Ideology and Student Activism

Introduction

A major alternative approach to student activism than the approach stressing radical political consciousness is one that stresses reformist political consciousness. Various theorists have seen students attempting to obtain some type of social reform, as distinct from more radical change. This chapter considers two of the most important theories of activism that focus on reformist ideology. First, we examine the role of civil rights ideology in activism, and then we analyze the impact of educational reform ideology on activism.

Theorists such as Pinkney have enunciated the role of civil rights ideology in generating student activism.[1] Civil rights ideology focuses on attempts to improve conditions of ethnic minorities, especially blacks, *within* existing social-economic arrangements. An important comparison to the black revolutionary movement is the Civil Rights Movement. As classically stated, civil rights ideology stressed that democracy, integration, freedom, and equality for blacks were possible within the basic framework of American society. Civil rights ideology argued that various institutions such as the economy, education, and politics had to be internally reformed to include people of all races on equal basis. But the general feeling among participants in the movement was that American society could do this.[2] In comparison, the black revolutionary movement rejects this assumption. We will examine the association between attachment to classic civil rights ideology and activism in the latter part of the Sixties. Even if there were evidence of a strong positive association between these variables in the early part of the Sixties, did the association still hold at the end of the decade?

The second type of reformist theory of activism to be examined here involves students considered as a group. The concern is with the extent to which alienation from the university is associated with student activism. Students have been seen as rebelling, not for wider political-economic aims such as the overthrow of capitalism, but in response to their own lowly status in the university. It is felt that their political actions are parallel to those of labor unions: they resent the more powerful university administration or faculty, and therefore aim their political actions at improving their conditions "at the factory." Mario Savio and Paul Goodman, among others, have argued this viewpoint, and Joseph Schwab developed a theory of activism that emphasizes the role of poor educational conditions in understanding activism.[3]

Civil rights ideology and educational reform ideology are being separately considered in this chapter because by the end of the Sixties they had different relations to activism. As a result, we have not put them together into an overall index of reformist political consciousness similar to our overall index of radical political consciousness. In general, there is some evidence supporting the reformist approach to activism, but the evidence is weaker than for our own approach emphasizing radical political consciousness.

Civil Rights Ideology and Student Activism

In general, a radical versus reformist position on civil rights involves: (1) a belief in the necessity to make changes *of* versus *within* such social systems as the economic system and legal system to achieve civil rights goals or (2) the advocacy of violent versus non-violent means to achieve civil rights goals. Those who advocate either changes of the social system or the use of violent means to achieve civil rights goals are considered radicals on the civil rights issue; those who advocate changes in the system by non-violent means are considered reformists on this issue. We usually do not use choice of "means" to delineate political positions. However, the use of non-violence was so much a part of the philosophy of Martin Luther King that it required inclusion in our definition of civil rights ideology.[4]

The single most important finding in this study with regard to civil rights ideology and student activism is that by 1968 there was a moderate *negative* relationship between these variables of e = -15 percent (see Table 11-1)—that is, the more the student adhered to classic civil rights ideology, the less likely he was to be involved in activism. This means that the more likely a student adhered to the classic position that non-violent actions can lead to equality for Negroes, the less likely he was to be an activist.

This type of finding contrasts sharply with Pinkney's finding of a very strong positive relationship between classic civil rights views and activism in 1963-64. In Pinkney's study, 94 percent felt racial equality was possible, and 77 percent supported non-violent resistance; only 11 percent favored armed self-defense as a civil rights tactic.[5] Similarly, the large majority of Pinkney's respondents felt reformist measures such as legislation and community self-help would be sufficient to generate equality.[6] But by 1968, our data indicate a negative relationship between civil rights ideology and activism, at least for students at Berkeley.

Some comments should be made on this finding. In order to avoid

Table 11-1
Student's Civil Rights Ideology and Student Activism

Student Activism	Student's Civil Rights Ideology		
	High	Low	
Active	(95) 28%	(41) 43%	$e = -15\%$ $\chi^2 = .01$
Total	(342) 100%	(95) ⋅100%	

Table 11-2
Student Activism and Student's Civil Rights Ideology

Student's Civil Rights Ideology	Student Activism		
	Active	Non-active	
High	(95) 70%	(247) 82%	$e = -12\%$
Low	(41) 30%	(54) 18%	$\chi^2 = .01$
Total	(136) 100%	(301) 100%	

misleading the reader, it should be pointed out that the majority of activists are actually high rather than low on civil rights ideology (see Table 11-2). However, non-activists are even more likely to be high than low on civil rights ideology. Thus, the finding that activists are more likely to be high than low on civil rights ideology does not tell us much about activism. There remains an inverse relationship between these variables.

In addition, it is worth mentioning the percentage of people who are high on civil rights ideology that are also high on liberal versus radical ideology. It might be expected that those who are high on civil rights ideology would be more likely to be high on liberal ideology than radical ideology. In fact, this is the case, but the difference found is not large. Seventy-six percent of those who are high on civil rights ideology are also high on liberal ideology, whereas 68 percent of those who are high on civil rights ideology are also high on radical ideology. Thus, civil rights ideology is somewhat more associated with general liberal ideology than with radical ideology, but the difference is not accentuated.

This finding should be considered with the two previous findings that a moderate inverse relation exists between civil rights ideology and activism but that the numerical majority of activists are high rather than low on civil rights ideology. The upshot of all these findings is that civil rights ideology tends to reflect a politically moderate position in the realms of ideas and action. But also the findings show that radical ideas and radical actions are by no means incompatible with classic civil rights views concerning the use of non-violent means to achieve freedom and equality for blacks. Thus, a person might want to make basic changes of the social system to achieve freedom and equality for blacks, even using non-institutionalized means to do so, but he still could be committed to non-violence. Of course, as findings presented below indicate, he could also be committed to violence. But a commitment to radical change is not incompatible with a commitment to the use of non-violent methods.

Furthermore, the inverse relationship between civil rights ideology and student activism does not imply that white student activists by 1968 had somehow severed their ties with the Third World movement.[7] On the contrary. Even though an inverse relationship existed between classic civil rights ideology and activism, a strong positive relationship existed between activism and support for Black Power ideology. However, in Chapter 3 it was noted that Black Power ideology was involved in a *radical* critique of the racist system in the U.S.

Finally, there was a positive association between activism and the view that equality for blacks could be obtained through violence. This finding suggests that some activists in the latter part of the 1960s felt equality was still possible for blacks but that they changed their minds on the possibility of non-violence securing that goal.[8] In sum, by 1968 in Berkeley, activism was positively associated with the radical aspects of Third World ideology, but negatively associated with reformist aspects of this ideology. Hence reformist views on civil rights should not be seen as an underlying condition of activism by the late Sixties.

Educational Reform Ideology and Student Activism

In trying to understand why students engaged in protests in the Sixties, the "multiversity" was frequently mentioned as a major source of the protests. Students were seen as acting in response to their criticisms of conditions in the multiversity, and in response to their desires for university reform. Thus, we will be most interested in the relationship between activism and students' views about such issues as class size, student control over their

Table 11-3
Student's Educational Reform Ideology and Student Activism

Student Activism	Student's Educational Reform Ideology		
	High	Low	
Active	(115) 35%	(22) 20%	e = 15% χ^2 = .01
Total	(328) 100%	(109) 100%	

education, student evaluation of the faculty, the view that professors are more interested in research than teaching, the idea that U. C. Berkeley is a "factory," student opinion that they can or cannot count on the U. C. faculty or administration, and general student satisfaction with the Berkeley campus. An index of educational reform ideology is formed by selecting from these issues and is reported in detail in Appendix C. We use it to see the impact of educational ideology on participation in activism.

There is a positive relationship between this index of student's educational reform ideology and student activism of e = 15 percent, which is statistically significant by the Chi-Square test at the .01 level (see Table 11-3). Although this initial relationship between student's educational reform ideology and activism is not as strong as the initial relationship between student's radical ideology and activism of e = 29 percent with a Chi-Square of .001, there is some support for the view that activists were protesting educational conditions perceived to be inadequate.

It would be interesting at this point to introduce a series of third variables that related to the *objective* educational situation of activists. These objective conditions would include actual large-size classes, professors who were truly more interested in research than teaching, actual bureaucratic treatment of students, and so forth. Then we could see whether those students who really did experience poor educational conditions *perceived* these conditions as bad and then engaged in activism as a result. Unfortunately, we do not have questionnaire data on the objective educational conditions of the students; we only have data on students' perceptions of their educational circumstances. So it is difficult to examine with our questionnaire data a hypothesis focusing on possible links between objective educational conditions, perceived educational conditions, and student activism.

However, instead of postponing any investigation of the sources of educational criticism for "future research," we can examine one type of

Table 11-4
Parents' Educational Reform Ideology and Student Activism

	Parent		
	Father		
Student Activism	*Educational Reform Ideology*		
	High	*Low*	
Active	(8)	(46)	e = 6%
	40%	34%	χ^2 = N.S.
Total	(20)	(134)	
	100%	100%	
	Mother		
Student Activism	*Educational Reform Ideology*		
	High	*Low*	
Active	(7)	(55)	e = 10%
	44%	34%	χ^2 = N.S.
	(16)	(163)	
	100%	100%	

hypothesis with our data. There is an alternative hypothesis to the theory that objective educational conditions lead to perceived inadequacies in education, which in turn lead to student activism. The alternative hypothesis would argue that educational criticisms were learned in the family and that these educational criticisms later get translated into student activism. We do have information on the links between parental views of education at Berkeley, the student's view of education at Berkeley, and student activism.

Tables 11-4 and 11-5 indicate that the predicted links between parental views of education at Berkeley, the student's view of education at Berkeley, and student activism do not occur. Table 11-4 shows only a very modest initial relationship between educational reform ideology of the parents and student activism. Following the procedures outlined in Chapter 4 for "interpreting" this initial relationship, we would introduce student's educational reform ideology as a third variable. In order for the expected interpretation to occur, the initial positive relationship would have to drop in all partial tables or become accentuated under the condition

Table 11-5

Parents' Educational Reform Ideology and Student Activism, with Student's Educational Reform Ideology Controlled

Student's Educational Reform Ideology

	High			*Low*		
Student Activism	*Father's Ed. Ref. Ideology*			*Father's Ed. Ref. Ideology*		
	High	*Low*		*High*	*Low*	
Active	(7) 44%	(37) 37%	$e = 7\%$ $\chi^2 = $ N.S.	(1) 25%	(9) 26%	$e = -1\%$ $\chi^2 = $ N.S.
Total	(16) 100%	(99) 100%		(4) 100%	(35) 100%	

Student's Educational Reform Ideology

	High			*Low*		
Student Activism	*Mother's Ed. Ref. Ideology*			*Mother's Ed. Ref. Ideology*		
	High	*Low*		*High*	*Low*	
Active	(5) 38%	(47) 38%	$e = 0\%$ $\chi^2 = $ N.S.	(2) 67%	(8) 20%	$e = 47\%$ $\chi^2 = .10$
Total	(13) 100%	(122) 100%		(3) 100%	(41) 100%	

of high educational reform ideology of the student. As Table 11-5 indicates, neither of these results occurs for either parent. Thus, we must conclude that educational reform ideology of the parents is not a general source of a student's educational reform ideology and participation in activism.

What we have done by the following procedure is eliminate a major alternative hypothesis to the theory that objective educational conditions give rise to subjective perceptions of educational conditions, which are associated with student activism. We have shown that family educational ideology is not strongly associated with student educational ideology and activism. This "argument by elimination" lends some support to the theory stressing objective educational conditions and activism—that is, if the source of activists' educational ideology is not family educational ideology, then it could be objective educational conditions that give rise to student ideology and activism.

Instead of further pursuing this particular relationship between student educational reform ideology and activism, the next chapter examines educational ideology in the context of objective educational conditions and radical political ideology. We show that the likelihood of activism increases among students who are critical of their education *and* critical of the larger society. In fact, educational ideology—independent of a commitment to radical ideology—is not a very strong determinant of participation in activism. Thus, we must conclude that there is some limited evidence of the impact of reform ideology on activism, but the impact is clearly weaker than the impact of radical ideology.

Notes

1. Alphonso Pinkney, *The Commited: White Activists in the Civil Rights Movement* (New Haven: College and University Press, 1968). Civil rights protest was involved in one of our items of student activism —participation in the Free Speech Movement. The FSM began over collection of funds for the civil rights organization, CORE.

2. Ibid., pp. 138, 146-47.

3. Mario Savio, "An End to History," in Seymour Martin Lipset and Sheldon S. Wolin, eds., *The Berkeley Student Revolt* (Garden City, N.Y.: Anchor Books, 1965), pp: 216-19; Joseph J. Schwab, *College Curriculum and Student Protest* (Chicago: The University of Chicago Press, 1969); Paul Goodman, "Thoughts on Berkeley," *The New York Review of Books* III, No. 11 (January 14, 1965):5-6.

4. Martin Luther King, Jr., *Stride Toward Freedom: The Montgomery Story* (New York: Harper & Brothers, 1958); Martin Luther King, Jr., *Where Do We Go From Here: Chaos or Community?* (New York: Harper & Row, 1967).

5. Pinkney, op. cit., pp. 138, 146.

6. Ibid., p. 147, Table 12.

7. The large majority of students in our sample are white.

8. It should be noted that the student respondent was presented with two separate questions; one asked whether non-violence would produce equality for blacks and the other asked whether violence would produce equality for blacks. Thus, the respondent could feel equality will come from non-violence, violence, both conditions, or neither condition.

12

The New Working Class and Student Activism

Theoretical Perspective

Near the end of the Sixties a new type of explanation of activism began to emerge within the New Left movement itself. Influenced by recent European ideas along the same lines, various American thinkers argued that a New Working Class of educated laborers was developing in advanced corporate capitalist society.[1] Parallel to Marx's ideas about the Old Working Class of industrial workers, the New Working Class was seen as alienated and exploited by capitalism. However, instead of traditional factory conditions producing this alienation and exploitation, conditions in the modern university and modern economy were seen to have similar results for educated workers. Eventually educated workers recognize they are alienated and exploited. As a result, they develop a simultaneous radical criticism of corporate capitalism and the educational system that is a part of this economic structure. Hence, the educated workers are seen to participate in various political protests against the educational and economic systems of corporate capitalism.

There are at least two branches of New Working Class theory. One focuses specifically on the educational conditions of corporate capitalist society; the other focuses on those who have been trained in this educational system but who are now working in capitalist bureaucracies.[2] Our concern is primarily with the educational circumstances of the capitalist multiversity—that is, the political ideas and actions students develop in response to the presumed oppressive educational conditions in the universities of advanced capitalism.

There are various ways that the educational system has been pictured as exploiting and alienating students. For example, it is argued that the end product of education—technical knowledge—is for a later employer, not for the student himself. In addition, it is charged that students do not view education as an end in itself, but only as a means to avoid other forms of oppression such as unemployment and the military draft (when such a draft is in operation). As a result, students must be motivated by rewards and punishments such as grades and threats of failure that are external to the learning process. Capitalist education has even been seen as a "full-time but unpaid job," with all the connotations of exploitation.[3] In fact, modern capitalism is seen as using the educational system to absorb its own "surplus labor." And if surplus laborers decide not to continue with school, then they face serious possibilities of unemployment. But even when they stay in school, educated laborers are seen to get fewer and fewer benefits from their education.

New Working Class theorists feel the educational system must repress the interests of students and orient the students to the needs of bureaucratic capitalism. Thus, any type of creativity on the part of students that does not fit into the technical expertise required by capitalism must be suppressed. Certainly any creativity that questioned existing political-economic arrangements should be stifled. The modern economic system is seen as needing highly trained and specialized personnel to run the complex capitalist economy. This means the university should stick to such duties as training thousands of scientists and engineers, professionals of every sort, and bureaucratic managers who can relate to these technical employees. Hence, it is argued that the needs of the capitalist economy dictate what is to be taught by the university , who teaches it, and what type of students should ultimately be "produced" by the "knowledge factory."

Due to university involvement with the capitalist system, New Working Class theorists see the university cooperating with various repressive institutions. In particular, the university is seen as cooperating with the military draft. During the Sixties, many universities did give out class rankings and grade point averages of students with the knowledge that these would be used to draft students to fight in Vietnam (as well as provide others with exemptions). In fact, some demonstrations occurred with specific regard to the draft and class rankings (e.g., at the University of Chicago).[4] Hence the draft—and the university's complicity with the draft—was seen as an important source of radicalization by New Working Class theorists.

It is clear that New Working Class theory focuses on a group of people who have previously been described as rather conservative or moderate in their political outlook because they were being prepared to hold *favored* positions in the economic system. The educational system, according to this more traditional view, was seen as the avenue of social mobility for those who aspired to middle- or even upper-class positions. Certainly the educational system was not thought of as a source of discontent. However, New Working Class theory offers a challenge to this older interpretation of the university as it relates to the student and the larger society.

We can empirically examine some of the basic propositions of New Working Class theory and see that it can predict a type of political ideology adhered to by many activists. This is an ideology that simultaneously criticizes the educational system and the larger social system. Gintis feels that radical student ideology must criticize both capitalism and the educational system, support "student power," and be " . . . anti-racist, equalitarian, and anti-imperialist as well as anti-repressive and anti-alienative."[5] Since this ideology involves both a radical opposition to the larger social system and a support for educational reforms, we refer to this ideology as a radical-reformist political consciousness. Although New Working Class theory points to the role of this type of ideology in activism, other weaker aspects of the theory make it a less convincing theory of activism than our own approach stated earlier.

An Empirical Test of the New Working Class Theory of Activism

One of the basic assumptions of the New Working Class theory of student activism is that the modern university is closely tied into the existing "Establishment" and consciously serves the needs of the larger society. Ever since Clark Kerr published *The Uses of the University*, it has been clear that universities like U. C. Berkeley do in fact serve existing political, economic, and military institutions.[6] However, the Rowntrees' assertion that "the university is a wholly-owned subsidiary of the war machine" is an overstatement.[7] Universities not only support the existing society, but they also nurture a critical attitude toward various social arrangements.[8] Thus, the assumption concerning the relationship of the university to the larger society has some validity, but the Rowntrees have overstated the degree of subservience of the university to the larger society.

There are other aspects of New Working Class theory that have some validity, but such assertions are likely to be overstatements as in the following situations:

1. Knowledge in the university is dominated by economic considerations. Although much knowledge in the university has some occupational relevance for the student, the university is also a source of criticism of the economic system, and the university does offer many courses that have few clearcut ties to capitalism (e.g., courses in the humanities).

2. The student must be motivated by rewards extrinsic to the learning process such as grades and job possibilities. Although this may be the case for various students, there are other students who are quite involved in their studies for their own sake.

3. Education is a full-time, but unpaid job. Although there is something to this argument in view of the hours the student must spend in preparation for his studies, which are unpaid if he does not have some financial aid while in school, many students do have some financial aid, and in any case, the status of an unpaid worker usually is quite short-termed for most students.

4. The educational system keeps students off the labor market, even to the extent that this leads to the formation of youth societies that foster student activism. Although being in school does to some extent keep young adults off the labor market, this only lasts for a limited number of years for each student, and even those students who remain in school for extended periods do not necessarily become part of genuine "youth societies," such as Isla Vista in Santa Barbara; many activists have little or nothing to do with actual youth societies.

There are still other aspects of New Working Class theory that are often undocumented and seem doubtful at best; for example:

1. Universities such as U. C. Berkeley are generally repressive institutions. At most it would be possible to argue that the university upholds campus regulations, but it also permits a great range of activities for students, including political activities.
2. The student's interests are opposite of and antagonistic to the interests of the university, which thereby necessitates the previously mentioned repressive education in capitalist society. A central problem with this formulation is the failure of the theorists to clearly delineate the "interests" of the students and the university; without a clear specification of the interests of the parties involved, it is difficult to make a judgment concerning this proposition.
3. The university exploits and alienates students in a Marxist sense. Although a few limited groups of students, such as teaching assistants, probably are exploited in the university, the other discussions of student alienation and exploitation are pretty general and rather undocumented. Probably the discussions of alienation emphasizing certain separations for the student (e.g., the separation for some students between the learning process and the external rewards for learning) are better than the discussions of student exploitation; but New Working Class theory, if it is to provide an adequate Marxist analysis of the university, must develop greater conceptual clarity and empirical documentation for the key ideas of student alienation and exploitation.

Although we have suggested modification or rejection for some aspects of New Working Class theory, our data provide confirmation for at least some other aspects of the theory. The relations between radical political ideology, educational criticisms, and student activism constitute an important part of the theory of Gintis and the Rowntrees. They argue that radical ideology, educational criticisms, and student activism are all derived from the objective conditions of the student status. Following Gintis and the Rowntrees, we would expect that the combination of radical political consciousness and educational reform consciousness would be more highly associated with student activism than either radical consciousness

Table 12-1
Student's Radical-Reformist Political Consciousness and Student Activism

	Student's Radical Political Consciousness		
	High		
Student Activism	Student's Educational Reform Consciousness		
	High	*Low*	
Active	(81) 49%	(8) 36%	e = 13% χ^2 = N.S.
Total	(165) 100%	(22) 100%	
	Low		
Student Activism	Student's Educational Reform Consciousness		
	High	*Low*	
Active	(34) 21%	(14) 16%	e = 5% χ^2 = N.S.
Total	(163) 100%	(87) 100%	

or educational reform consciousness alone. Table 12-1 indicates that this is in fact the case. There is a steady increase in association with student activism as we move from low radical consciousness and low educational reform consciousness to high radical consciousness and high educational reform consciousness, as would be predicted from New Working Class theory.

In previous chapters, we have introduced third variables in order to replicate, explain away, interpret, or specify some initial two-variable relationship. However, there can be an additional function of adding a third variable. Rosenberg notes that adding a third variable to the original two-variable relationship may have the function of seeing how two separate independent variables affect a common dependent variable.[9] He says: "In this case the third variable is not a test factor in the usual sense but is rather seen as another independent variable."[10] Thus, we can see the *additive* effect of two independent variables on one dependent variable when we introduce a third variable. We might note that the logical structure of the theory involved dictates when the analyst looks for this type of additive effect rather than the more common types of elaboration such as interpretation, and specification. In sum, Table 12-1 shows the additive effect of radical political consciousness and educational reformist political consciousness on student activism.

Table 12-1 also makes clear that those who are only high on educational reform consciousness are not too likely to be student activists. The reader is referred to Chapter 11 where the relationship between educational ideology and student activism is discussed. The finding here that educational ideology, apart from radical ideology, is not highly associated with activism should be taken as a conclusion to the discussion of educational ideology and activism in Chapter 11. However, if a student is only high on radical political consciousness, he is definitely more likely to be an activist than if he is only high on educational reform consciousness. But student activism is involved with the university in many ways; thus there is a still greater likelihood of activism when a student is critical of the educational system as well as the larger social system. One final point on this issue: Table 12-1 indicates that only 22 students are high on radical consciousness and low on educational reform consciousness and that only 8 are activists. Thus, if a student is high on radical consciousness (at least at Berkeley in 1968), he will also be likely to criticize the educational system and want educational changes. All of these facts are consistent with predictions from New Working Class theory about ideological tendencies among activists.[11]

Our data contain other items that relate to ideas suggested by New Working Class theory. Both activists and students high on radical political consciousness strongly felt that the University of California at Berkeley was too closely tied to the existing political-economic "Establishment." This type of sentiment would be predicted by the theory of the new working class, that is, the university is looked at by activists as too involved with corporate capitalism.

However, contrary to predictions from New Working Class theory, activists are by no means fully estranged from the university. Our data clearly reject the proposition that activists, or those radically conscious, would drop out of school if it were not for the military draft or unemployment. A very large majority of activists and non-activists, as well as those high versus low on radical political consciousness, would be attending school even if they were not faced with the draft or unemployment. Thus, the University of California at Berkeley has various positive attractions to activists in spite of their criticisms of the university's role in the larger society.

Furthermore, there is at least suggestive evidence in Chapters 6 and 8 that the university is of less importance than the family in producing radical

Table 12-2
Student's Draft Status and Student Activism

	Student's Draft Status			
Student Activism	I-A	II-S	Not Eligible	
Active	(8) 67%	(53) 37%	(18) 28%	dyx = .141 χ^2 = .05
Total	(12) 100%	(144) 100%	(65) 100%	

consciousness and student activism. Chapter 6 indicated that the parents of only a minority of U. C. Berkeley students reported changes in their basic values since attending Berkeley. In addition, our data show that changes in values at Berkeley are not too strongly associated with student activism. New Working Class theory would predict much stronger relations between university experience, the development of radical-reformist political consciousness, and student activism. As such, there is evidence against the theory. Finally, there is suggestive evidence in Chapter 8 that points to the following proposition: the university may act as a radicalizing and activating agent especially for students from culturally unconventional family backgrounds. Thus, it may be necessary to combine the New Working Class theory with the family-cultural focus in order to see the role of the university in student activism. Although this is a tentative conclusion, university experience may serve to generate radical political consciousness and student activism particularly for students from unconventional cultural backgrounds. But university experience may not have the same radicalizing and activating effects for students in general, as would be predicted from New Working Class theory.

The military draft, however, had the predicted effects. Those most threatened with being drafted were the most likely to be student activists. There is a steady increase in the likelihood of activism when one compares students ineligible for the draft to those with temporary deferments (II-S status) to those immediately available for induction into the army (I-A status) (see Table 12-2).

Furthermore, we wanted to see whether there were links between draft status, radical political consciousness, and student activism—that is, whether radical consciousness interpreted the original relation between student's draft status and student activism. As Table 12-3 indicates, there is some evidence for and against the hypothesis that the student's draft status is associated with radical consciousness and student activism. On one hand, it is hard to make a case for interpretation when the entire table is

Table 12-3
Student's Draft Status and Student Activism, with Student's Radical Political Consciousness Controlled

Student's Radical Political Consciousness

High

Student's Draft Status

Student Activism	I-A	II-S	Not Eligible	
Active	(3) 60%	(36) 54%	(10) 38%	dyx = .148 χ^2 = N.S.
Total	(5) 100%	(66) 100%	(26) 100%	

Low

Student's Draft Status

Student Activism	I-A	II-S	Not Eligible	
Active	(5) 71%	(17) 22%	(8) 20%	dyx = .116 χ^2 = .02
Total	(7) 100%	(78) 100%	(39) 100%	

considered—that is, when radical political consciousness is introduced as the third variable, there is not a reduction in all partial tables of the original relationship or a significant increase in the original relationship under the condition of high radical consciousness (the original relation of dyx = .141 decreases to dyx = .116 under the condition of low radical consciousness and increases slightly to dyx = .148 under the condition of high radical consciousness). However, there is a significant increase in proportion activist for students with a II-S draft status (originally 37 percent of students with a II-S draft status were activists, and this increased to 54 percent under the condition of high radical consciousness). So it is possible to argue that the draft status of II-S was associated with radical political consciousness and student activism.

Since many activists had a II-S draft status, it is important to understand the radicalizing effects of this status on students. Although the II-S status temporarily protected students from fighting in Vietnam, it was an uncertain status that usually had to be renewed each year. In this regard, various draft officials, especially General Lewis Hershey, often threatened to abolish the II-S status in order to draft students.[12] In fact, the status was eventually abolished. Thus, many anxieties were aroused in students holding this status, even though they did not immediately have to participate in the war.

Even more deeply, a II-S draft status was involved in a questioning of basic values for many students. Open attempts to avoid fighting in Vietnam by using the II-S status brought up these questions of basic values because the student had to justify to himself and others why he was opposed to the war. In this situation, students often called into question the larger social system because they saw Vietnam as part of a broader imperialist strategy of the United States. Thus, students' interests and Vietnamese interests were threatened by the same system. In sum, New Working Class theory is able to explain many aspects of the relationship between the draft, radical political consciousness, and student activism.

Conclusion

We have empirically examined a rather complex theory of activism centering on the rise of a radicalized New Working Class of educated laborers in capitalist society. We have seen that this theory is much more elaborate than a theory focusing on educational discontents alone. The theory of the New Working Class does discuss educational discontents, but these discontents are tied into an analysis of education in advanced capitalist societies.

There are strong points to this theory. It accurately depicts the role of radical-reformist ideology in activism. We have seen that attachment to educational reform ideology, apart from attachment to radical ideology, does not have a strong impact on activism. Thus,New Working Class theory is a clear improvement on the theory of activism stressing educational discontents alone. Similarly, New Working Class theory is an improvement on a purely cultural theory of activism. If we recall, the addition of a student's unconventional cultural values to his or her radical ideology did not explain much more of the variation in activism. In contrast, the addition of educational reform ideology to radical ideology did explain more of the variation in activism.[13] In addition, New Working Class theory accurately predicted the effects of the military draft on activism. And the theory correctly asserted that many activists felt the university was too closely tied to the existing political-economic "Establishment."

However, there are various weak aspects of the New Working Class theory of activism. We have seen that two of its central concepts, student alienation and student exploitation, are rather weakly developed and documented. Also, the structural conditions it presumes are often questionable as they have been described in the theory. For example, the notion that a university like U. C. Berkeley is generally repressive requires reformulation. Similarly, New Working Class theory does not often delineate exactly how students' interests are opposite of university and capitalist interests. In fact, we saw that most activists would remain in school even if they were not threatened with unemployment or the draft, which is quite contrary to New Working Class theory.

In conclusion, we feel that New Working Class theory is especially helpful in pointing to the role of radical-reformist ideology in activism, and in showing how activism can be partly explained by university complicity with the draft. But due to various weaknesses of the theory, it cannot be considered as a complete explanation of activism. Thus, our approach, which focuses on activists responding to political events like Vietnam in terms of radical values derived from their parents' radical political or culturally unconventional values, would seem to be a stronger approach than one emphasizing capitalist education. In fact, data from past chapters on the cultural background of activists and on university socialization suggest that New Working Class theory may be especially relevant for students of unconventional cultural backgrounds, but not as relevant for students in general.

Notes

1. For discussions of New Working Class theory, see: Serge Mallet, *La Nouvelle Classe Ouvrière* (Paris: Éditions du Seuil, 1963); Herbert Gintis, "The New Working Class and Revolutionary Youth," *Continuum* 8 (Spring-Summer 1970): 151-74; John and Margaret Rowntree, "The Political Economy of Youth: Youth as Class," published by *The Radical Education Project*, Box 625, Ann Arbor, Michigan 48107, pp. 1-36 (it also appeared in *Our Generation*, Vol. 6, Nos. 1-2); Martin Oppenheimer, "White Collar Revisited: The Making of a New Working Class," *Social Policy* 1, No. 2 (July-August 1970): 27-32; Martin J. Sklar, "On the Proletarian Revolution and the End of Political-Economic Society," *Radical America* III, No. 3 (May-June 1969): 1-41; Bogdan Denitch, "Is There a 'New Working Class'?," *Dissent* (July-August 1970): 351-5; Richard Flacks, "Young Intelligentsia in Revolt," *Trans-action* (June 1970): 47-55; Samuel R. Friedman, "Perspectives on the American Student Movement," *Social Problems* 20, No. 3 (Winter 1973): 283-99. Probably the first statement of New Working Class theory was by Veblen when he discussed the radical potential of engineers. See Thorstein Veblen, *The Engineers and the Price System* (New York: The Viking Press, 1921, 1932). For an excellent criticism of New Working Class theory, see Stanley Aronowitz, "Does the

United States Have a New Working Class?,'' in George Fischer, ed., *The Revival of American Socialism* (New York: Oxford University Press, 1971), Chapter 10, pp. 188-216.

2. Some theorists, such as Friedman, op. cit., attempt to integrate the two branches of New Working Class theory, and most discussions have something to say about both aspects of the theory. But they are distinct focuses within the same general theoretical framework.

3. Rowntree, op. cit., p. 14.

4. Richard Flacks, ''The Liberated Generation: An Exploration of the Roots of Student Protest,'' *The Journal of Social Issues* 23 (July 1967): 52-75; and Jerome H. Skolnick, *The Politics of Protest* (New York: Ballantine Books, 1969), pp. 47-49.

5. Gintis, op. cit., pp. 152, 169.

6. Clark Kerr, *The Uses of the University* (Cambridge, Mass.: Harvard University Press, 1964).

7. Rowntree, op. cit., p. 28.

8. For a discussion of the dual roles of the university, see Seymour Martin Lipset, *Rebellion in the University* (Boston: Little, Brown & Co., 1972), p. 31.

9. Morris Rosenberg, *The Logic of Survey Analysis* (New York: Basic Books, 1968), Chapter 7, ''Conjoint Influence,'' pp. 159-65.

10. Ibid., p. 159.

11. Neil J. Smelser of the Department of Sociology at the University of California, Berkeley has noted in a private communication that these findings are also consistent with other positions besides New Working Class theory.

12. Skolnick, op. cit., pp. 95, 322.

13. In our data, the ideological group that is most likely of all to be activists are those who are high on radical political consciousness, high on educational reform ideology, and low on civil rights ideology; 66 percent of these people are activists.

13 The Development, Decline, and Renewal of Student Activism

Introduction

Previous chapters have focused on middle-range theories of activism rather than on macroscopic approaches to activism.[1] Our own theory of activitism, enunciated in Chapter 2, is certainly a middle-range theory of activism, which focuses on the relationship between a limited set of variables. We indicated the strength of our own approach to activism in comparison with other middle-range theories that had less support. However, all middle-range theories have some difficulty explaining two phenomenon related to activism: (1) the participation of huge numbers of students in protest activities by the time of the Cambodian invasion in 1970 and (2) the decline of activism by 1973.[2] As a result, it is necessary to go beyond the middle-range approach to activism and employ a broader theoretical perspective to explain these phenomenon.

More generally, using a broader perspective permits us to explain changes in three main phases of the movement—its development, decline, and renewal. In addition, to give an historical focus to our study, we compare the student movement of the 1960s with the student movement of the 1930s. Similar general conditions led to the development of both movements, and both movements declined when certain necessary conditions were reduced in intensity. The general theoretical perspective and these historical comparisons permit us to make a prognosis about the future of activism in the United States.

A Theory of Collective Behavior

One broader theoretical perspective that can be used to analyze student activism is Neil J. Smelser's theory of collective behavior discussed in his *Theory of Collective Behavior,* and in his article "Social and Psychological Dimensions of Collective Behavior."[3] Smelser lists six conditions that are necessary conditions of collective behavior and that when combined at the same time and place constitute a sufficient condition of collective behavior. Synthesizing both of Smelser's discussions, we feel that the six conditions should be examined at the social and psychological levels of analysis. Most middle-range theories only focus on one or two of Smelser's six conditions.

143

Thus, the conditions in the middle-range theories must combine with the other conditions in Smelser's theory in order for them to influence student activism.

We take the following social and psychological conditions to be necessary conditions of engagement in collective behavior, and when they are combined at the same time and place, they constitute a sufficient condition of engagement in collective behavior:

1. *Structural conduciveness* or the permissiveness of social arrangements and personality systems to generate engagement in collective behavior.
2. *Structural strain* or the existence of ambiguities, deprivations, conflicts, and discrepancies in the social order. From the standpoint of the individual, structural strain refers to perceived deprivations, tensions, ambiguities, conflicts, and discrepancies.
3. *Growth and spread of generalized beliefs* or the existence in the population of beliefs that identify the source of strain, attribute certain characteristics to the source, and specify certain responses to the potential participants. From the standpoint of the individual, this determinant refers to the person being readied for action by attachment to these social beliefs.
4. *Precipitating factors* or the occurrence of some type of specific event that gives the generalized beliefs concrete substance. From the standpoint of the individual, this determinant refers to the individual perceiving this event as a threat to cherished values.
5. *Mobilization of participants for action* or the organization of the affected group into action. From the standpoint of the individual, this determinant refers to the availability of the individual to be recruited into the activity.
6. *The ineffective operation of controls* or the ineffectiveness of the social counter-determinants that prevent, interrupt, or inhibit the accumulation of the other five determinants of collective behavior. From the standpoint of the individual, this determinant refers to the lessening of personal controls, for example, because the actions are viewed as "morally correct." In addition, the combination of harshness and weakness by authorities aggravates instances of collective behavior.

The various specific conditions that we discussed in the previous chapters are in the nature of contributing conditions of activism, not necessary or sufficient conditions.[4] However, the determinants in Smelser's theory are necessary conditions of collective behavior. Furthermore, when there is evidence of these conditions occurring simultaneously, we would expect an instance of collective behavior to result. Many of our findings amount to specific types of evidence of generalized beliefs, structural conduciveness, etc. As such, they are examples of Smelser's six general conditions of collective behavior. But few, if any, of the specific conditions would be absolute requirements of student activism. Thus, generalized beliefs of some kind are required for an occurrence of student activism, but political consciousness is only a contributing condition of activism. Also, precipitating factors of some kind are required for student activism, but the police coming on campus is only a contributing condition of activism. Similarly, conduciveness at the social system level is required for engagement in activism, but large campus size only contributes to student activism. Examples could be multiplied. But it should be clear that Smelser's determinants of collective behavior are necessary conditions of activism, and when combined amount to a sufficient condition of activism. However, the specific instances of these conditions that we discuss only contribute to activism.

This reasoning is consistent with the logic of Smelser's primary methodology in *Theory of Collective Behavior*—namely, the methodology of systematic comparative illustration.[5] Our findings amount to systematic illustrations of the general conditions of collective behavior. In addition, Smelser's theory is falsifiable with the use of our data. If there are examples of each of Smelser's six determinants of collective behavior—examined at the social and psychological levels—and there is no occurrence of student activism, then we would take this as evidence against the theory. Also, if student activism occurred, but there were only three of the six determinants of collective behavior operating at the same time and place, we would similarly take this as evidence against the theory. Of course, when the six determinants are simultaneously in operation and an instance of student activism occurs, then we would count this as evidence for the theory. Finally, if only one to five of the determinants is in operation, and there is no student activism, then we would count this as evidence for the theory. In the following sections, Smelser's theory is used to help explain the development, decline, and renewal of student activism in the United States.

The Development of Activism

From the very modest beginnings in the late Fifties, the New Left movement grew to the point where literally millions of students were involved in political protests before the movement waned. We have previously seen that by 1970, 60 percent of the U.S. student population had engaged in some form of student protest. In a student population of approximately 7 million, this means that over 4 million students took part in some protest.[6] Going back one year to 1969 (i.e., prior to the widespread Cambodian protests), we saw that 40 percent of the student population engaged in some form of protest. This means that nearly 3 million were involved in protests *prior* to Cambodia.

Not wanting to overestimate the numbers of students involved in protests of the Sixties, we should point out that somewhat fewer students specifically engaged in picketing. In 1969, 18 percent of the student population had picketed, which is about 1.25 million students. In 1970, 29 percent of the student population had picketed, which is over 2 million students.[7] Furthermore, we do not argue that our own middle-range theory of activism can account for the majority of these millions of student protesters. Our own theory focuses on non-institutionalized protests whereas the data just presented do *not* assume non-institutionalized protests. Even picketing may be quite legal and institutionalized when "parade permits" are obtained. Our theory focusing on unconventional family backgrounds pertains more to explaining activism such as takeover of university buildings, sit-ins, and illegal strikes. Smelser's more general theory of collective behavior is useful to account for the millions of protesters engaging in institutionalized and non-institutionalized protests in the late 1960s and early 1970s.

Here, the collective behavior is student protest, and the examples of the conditions of collective behavior are as follows. Structural conduciveness would be represented by the various structural conditions we have mentioned, such as left-wing families, poor educational conditions, and education in capitalist society. Structural strain would be represented by, for example, the tensions of draft-age men in the 1960s during the Vietnam War; the felt deprivations by ideological activists who desired broad social change, but who also saw various political and economic impediments to change; and finally, the types of family tensions and conflicts Feuer described. The growth and spread of generalized beliefs would be represented by the various left-wing ideologies in the New Left—reformist ideologies in the early 1960s and more radical, anti-capitalist ideologies of the late 1960s. There were many precipitating factors throughout the 1960s provided by university administrators, such as calling police on campus, and by the U.S. government escalating the war in Vietnam. Various organizations such as SNCC, CORE, and SDS, and other specific campus organizations spent a good deal of effort trying to mobilize students in the 1960s. Finally, when all the other conditions were met, there usually occurred some student activism because most campuses—even Berkeley—were not armed camps on a routine basis. When the other conditions were met, the social control was usually weak enough, at least for a short period, for there to be an occurrence of activism. And, as the condition of harshness and weakness in authority implies, activism tended to increase when police came on campus but did not use full force against the demonstrators.[8]

At the end of the Sixties and at the 1970 Cambodian invasion, all of these conditions in Smelser's theory were at intense levels, and they were perceived as such by the majority of college students at the time. It is likely that many of the variables in Smelser's theory *increased* in intensity over time. This would be particularly the case for the level of strain involved, the spread of anti-war beliefs,[9] the mobilization of students, and the number of precipitating factors. Smelser did not rely primarily on quantitative data to support his theory. Hence he did not try to devise, for example, ten-point scales for each of the conditions of collective behavior. However, if such scales existed, many of the variables we mentioned would have registered on the high part of the scale by the end of the Sixties. As a result, when conditions like strain and beliefs develop over a period of approximately ten years, it is possible to understand why huge numbers of students were involved in some type of protest by the late Sixties and early Seventies.

The activism of the Sixties was most closely approximated by the student activism in the United States in the 1930s. There have been student disturbances throughout U.S. history over such issues as poor cafeteria food, religious differences between students and the campus administration, and the general doctrine of *in loco parentis*.[10] What distinguished the protests of the Thirties and Sixties from other protests were the numbers of students involved, and a critique of the existing political-economic system by various protesters.[11]

Similar to the Sixties, the protests of the Thirties were truly widespread. In terms of membership in radical organizations, there were probably more students involved in the Thirties than the Sixties. The American Student Union (ASU) had approximately 20,000 dues-paying members by 1937-38.[12] In contrast, the Students for a Democratic Society (SDS) never claimed more than 7,000 dues-paying members, "with another 30,000 to 35,000 active participants in local chapters, out of a student population seven times that of the 1930s."[13]

However, more students engaged in actual protests in the Sixties than in the Thirties. "The demonstrations and strikes held on Peace Day in April 1935 are reported to have included 185,000 students out of a total population of a million."[14] If we take this figure as representing a high point in the movement of the Thirties, we see that the movement of the Sixties had more protesters numerically and proportionately. The 185,000 is, of course, fewer student protesters than the millions we have seen by the late Sixties. Also, 185,000 represents less than 20 percent of the college student population in the Thirties, which is a smaller proportion of students than the 60 percent involved at the height of the movement in the Sixties. Still, whatever their differences, the movements in the Thirties and Sixties were clearly widespread social movements.

The conditions underlying the movement of the Thirties were similar to those underlying the movement of the Sixties. At the height of the movement, there were many strains associated with the depression and the threat of worldwide fascism. There were also conducive social structures such as left-wing families, poor educational conditions, and the like. Also many radical—socialist and communist—beliefs permeated student populations such as that of City College in New York. Similarly, college administrators and foreign and domestic governments provided precipitating factors for the movement. As we stated, various organizations such as the American Student Union were important in mobilizing students of the Thirties. Finally, similar to the Sixties, when the other conditions were met some student activism was likely because campuses of the Thirties were not armed camps on a routine basis.[15] In sum, we can predict widespread student activism when all the six conditions in Smelser's theory are operating at high levels of intensity for the student population. This occurred in the 1930s and again in the 1960s.

The Decline of Activism

By 1973 most commentators had declared the New Left movement dead. Protests had been replaced by non-political concerns for many students in the United States. As a result, an important criticism of middle-range theories of activism developed. It was charged by critics such as Lipset that many middle-range theories of activism were inaccurate because the conditions they emphasized persisted in the 1970s, but activism declined.[16] Thus, the critics ask, how can a theory of activism that relies on left-wing families be correct when we know that activism has declined although there are still many left-wing families? Similarly, they point out that activism has declined although there are still problems with education in the multiversity; higher education still has links with corporate capitalism; and there are still permissive families.

On one hand, we would like to agree with these critics for pointing out the limitations of the middle-range approach to studying activism. The critics certainly have shown that the use of single factors in explaining something as complex as activism has serious pitfalls. It is clear that the single factors are not necessary or sufficient conditions of activism, as their proponents have often implied.

However, we disagree with the critics in that we feel many of the conditions discussed earlier do contribute to activism, even though they are not necessary or sufficient conditions of activism.[17] We certainly feel that variables such as radical political consciousness that are part of our analysis influence activism. But we also feel that these variables only contribute to participation in activism; they are not necessary or sufficient conditions of activism.

Furthermore, we feel that the various middle-range theories—including our own—should be put in the context of Smelser's theory of collective behavior in order to meet the criticism that activism has declined even though the conditions they emphasize persist. Here, we briefly show how the middle-range theories can be put into the context of Smelser's theory and thereby meet the criticism concerning the decline of activism.

The use of Smelser's theory puts the various middle-range theories into a context of other variables required for activism. Although we have shown the impact of unconventional families on student activism, we would not expect the socialization process alone to generate widespread protests. Similarly, we have shown some evidence that activism is influenced by the educational system in corporate capitalist society; by students' educational discontents; and to a limited extent by permissive families. However, using Smelser's theory, we would not expect the mere existence of corporate capitalism and its educational system to produce persistent activism. Nor would we expect widespread activism to be produced solely by parental laxity of discipline, or by professorial neglect of undergraduate students. All of these contributors to activism would have to combine with other conditions of collective behavior such as strain and precipitating factors in order for social conditions such as radical families to effect student protests.

Furthermore, when any of the six conditions are significantly reduced, we would expect a decline in collective behavior. Of primary importance to the movement of the Sixties is the withdrawal of U.S. land fighting in Vietnam. The end of land fighting has very much lowered the likelihood of (1) high strains on college students; (2) precipitating factors like war escalations; and (3) the growth and spread of radical beliefs centering on U.S. imperialism.[18] These are all essential conditions of collective behavior, and when any or all of them are reduced, we would expect a decline in activism. Hence, social conditions, such as left-wing families, education in corporate capitalist society, and educational discontents can persist, yet activism will decline due to a reduction of strains, precipitating factors, and the spread of radical beliefs.

The reduction of activism in the Thirties occurred when the various left-wing groups decided to support United States opposition to international fascism. As a result, these groups gave up their attempt to have the United States take a neutral or "peace" stand on the developing crisis in Europe. Instead they would support a U.S. war effort against fascism.[19]

This meant that radical beliefs focusing on the inherent corruption of the U.S. social system were temporarily suspended. Instead of the left-wing challenging capitalism, it joined in a common fight against fascism. Similarly, the abandoning of a peace commitment in the movement changed the type of incident that could serve as a precipitating factor for collective behavior. In particular, any move toward war mobilization by the United States would no longer be a precipitating factor that could crystallize various strains and radical beliefs. In addition, radical groups like the ASU became of less importance once the left sided with the U.S. government. Various conditions such as left-wing families, poor educational conditions, and strains associated with fascism persisted. But activism of the Thirties declined when some of the other necessary conditions of activism were significantly reduced.

In the Seventies, some of the conditions in our own theory of activism have persisted, but others have declined. There certainly remain politically radical and culturally unconventional families, as well as conflict in these families. But our theory also emphasized that students were acting on radical values in relation to political events such as Vietnam. The reduction of strains and precipitating factors associated with land fighting in Vietnam thus explains why some of the conditions we stressed persisted yet activism declined—that is, our middle-range theory stressed the importance of a student's generalized beliefs, as well as structurally conducive families, and strains associated with events such as Vietnam.[20] Hence, it is possible for the generalized beliefs and conducive families to persist and activism to decline because of a reduction in strains associated with Vietnam.[21]

The Renewal of Activism

This is not to say that the U.S. government and economy, as well as other major institutions, could not again produce new strains and precipitating factors, for example, by renewing land fighting in Asia. In fact, the U. C. Berkeley administration recently created a situation of strain for the students, which did culminate in renewed activism on a limited scale.[22] However, widespread renewed activism will probably have to await the production of new strains, precipitating factors, and mobilization efforts with regard to many U.S. students. Structural conditions and the level of control tend to remain roughly constant over time. In addition, there are always some students attached to left-wing political views, especially those who come from radical political or culturally unconventional backgrounds. But strains, precipitating factors, and political mobilization efforts are more variable. Hence, an increase in these latter factors will likely lead to renewed widespread activism in the United States because they can combine with the previous three necessary conditions of collective behavior.

In the near future we will probably not witness the widespread activism that occurred in the late 1960s. The government is not likely to hastily involve the United States in a war similar to Vietnam. However, we would predict activism to occur over specific injustices to ethnic minorities, women, and students in general. These protests will probably involve fewer students than in the late Sixties, and they may have more of a local than national focus. The two periods where the greatest amount of radical activism occurred in the United States, the 1930s and the 1960s, were also periods of great social crisis. It will probably take another crisis like the depression and threat of fascism in the Thirties and the Vietnam War in the Sixties to again produce the huge numbers of students involved in protests. Hence, the dramatic increase or decrease in U.S. student activism will be intimately linked to larger political-economic events.

Notes

1. For a discussion of middle-range theories, see Robert K. Merton, *Social Theory and Social Structure,* Revised and Enlarged Edition (London: The Free Press of Glencoe, Collier-Macmillan Limited, 1957, originally published in 1949), pp. 5-10. One of the few macroscopic approaches to explaining activism is found in Talcott Parsons and Gerald M. Platt, with the collaboration of Neil J. Smelser, *The American University* (Cambridge, Mass.: Harvard University Press, 1973).

2. Some people date the decline of activism as early as 1971. However Bayer and Astin clearly refute this position by presenting data on student activism for 1971. See Alan E. Bayer and Alexander W. Astin, "Campus Unrest, 1970-1971: Was It Really All That Quiet?," *Educational Record* 52 (Fall 1971): 301-13. In addition, there were short-lived protests at Berkeley in 1972 over U.S. activities in North Vietnam. But all agree that protests had declined by 1973.

3. Neil J. Smelser, *Theory of Collective Behavior* (New York: The Free Press of Glencoe, 1963); and Neil J. Smelser, "Social and Psychological Dimensions of Collective Behavior," in his *Essays in Sociological Explanation* (Englewood Cliffs, N.J.: Prentice-Hall, 1968), Chapter Five, pp. 92-121. Elsewhere we have employed Smelser's theory more elaborately to explain student activism in the United States. See James L. Wood, *Political Consciousness and Student Activism* (Beverly Hills: Sage Publications, in press).

4. A necessary condition implies that for Y to occur X must be present. A sufficient condition implies that every time X occurs Y will also occur. A contributing condition only implies that X and Y tend to be causally related; the existence of X tends to contribute to the existence of Y, but X is neither required nor sufficient for the existence of Y.

5. Smelser, *Theory of Collective Behavior,* op. cit., pp. 385-7.

6. The figure of 7 million for the student population in the 1960s is obtained from Seymour Martin Lipset and Everett Carll Ladd, Jr., "Col-

lege Generations—from the 1930s to the 1960s," *The Public Interest* 25 (Fall 1971): 103-4; and from a private communication from Seymour Martin Lipset, Department of Sociology and Department of Government, Harvard University, Cambridge, Massachusetts. The figure of 60 percent of American students involved in some type of protest by 1970 is obtained from Seymour Martin Lipset, *Rebellion in the University* (Boston: Little, Brown & Co., 1972), p. 45, Table 3; Lipset is citing data from "The Harris Survey."

7. These figures are derived from Lipset, ibid. For comparative figures in the 1968 French rebellion, it is estimated that at least 8 million students and workers took part in the protests. See Irwin M. Wall, "May 1968: When Students Spoke for France," *The Highlander* (student newspaper at the University of California, Riverside), p. 14.

8. For a discussion of the role of police in aggravating student protests, see Rodney Stark, *Police Riots: Collective Violence and Law Enforcement* (Belmont, California: Wadsworth Publishing Co., 1972).

9. As we have noted before, anti-war beliefs are not identical with radical beliefs. By the late Sixties there were opponents of the war from various political persuasions. There is evidence of an increase in both anti-war and radical beliefs in the student population throughout the Sixties, with anti-war beliefs increasing more so than specifically radical beliefs. See Lipset, *Rebellion in the University,* op. cit., p. 43, Table 2, and p. 49, Table 5.

10. For a discussion of various protests, see Lewis S. Feuer, *The Conflict of Generations* (New York: Basic Books, 1969), pp. 319-35.

11. Ibid., pp. 319-35, 353-73, and Chapters Eight and Nine, pp. 385-500.

12. Lipset and Ladd, op. cit., p. 103.

13. Ibid.

14. Ibid.

15. For discussions of activism in the 1930s, see Ibid., pp. 103-6; Feuer, op. cit., pp. 353-73; and Max Heirich and Sam Kaplan, "Yesterday's Discord," in Seymour Martin Lipset and Sheldon S. Wolin, eds., *The Berkeley Student Revolt* (Garden City, N. Y.: Anchor Books, 1965), pp. 10-17.

16. For example, in a private communication, Seymour Martin Lipset of Harvard University argued that structural conditions such as permissive families, education in capitalist society, left-wing families, and so forth persisted in the Seventies, but activism had declined. Hence the various middle-range theories of activism emphasizing these structural conditions could all be inaccurate.

17. For a discussion of necessary, sufficient, and contributing conditions, see note 4 of this chapter.

18. Lipset has also emphasized other conditions to account for the decline of activism. Besides the end of land fighting in Vietnam, he has included such factors as candidates for major political parties taking peace stands, the end of the period of assured jobs for college graduates, and college administrators using sophisticated social control tactics. See Seymour Martin Lipset, book review of Daniel Yankelovich, *The Changing Values on Campus: Political and Personal Attitudes of Today's College Students,* in *Change* 4 (November 1972): 60. While we agree about the importance of these factors, we also feel the end of land fighting in Vietnam is the most significant factor reducing strains on college students.

19. For discussions of the left-wing siding with U.S. opposition to fascism, see Lipset and Ladd, op. cit., p. 104; and Dwight Macdonald, *Memoirs of a Revolutionist* (New York: Farrar, Straus and Cudahy, 1957), pp. 113, 115.

20. Our middle-range theory did not emphasize precipitating factors, social control, or mobilization of students.

21. Lipset correctly states that strains on white students over civil rights were reduced when blacks took control of the movement. See Lipset's review of Yankelovich, op. cit., p. 60. However other strains on students persist (e.g., family tensions and conflicts). The fact that some strains persist points to a certain difficulty in Smelser's theory that makes it less determinate than it appears—that is, how are we to know which strains are the most important ones that will likely influence collective behavior? Earlier we stated that Smelser did not use a quantitative scale to measure his conditions of collective behavior. We suggest that devising such a scale would improve the theory because "cut-off" points could be set up to indicate when a given strain should contribute to collective behavior. As it is now, we only can only look for the existence of strains or the absence of strains. We should have specific guidelines to specify what *level* of a given strain would be expected to influence collective behavior.

22. The recent activism involved administrative threats to close down the popular School of Criminology at U. C. Berkeley. See "Police end UC campus protest," *Berkeley Daily Gazette,* Thursday, May 30, 1974, pp. 1-2; and Mark Trautwein, "UC's 'crim' protest growing," *Berkeley Daily Gazette,* Friday, May 31, 1974, pp. 1-2.

Appendixes

Appendix A
Discussion of
Questionnaires and
Surveys

The various theories of student activism are empirically tested by a secondary analysis of three instruments: two questionnaires and a Q-Sort. The items used from these instruments are reported in Appendix C. Dr. Robert H. Somers developed both questionnaires, and Dr. Jeanne Block and her associates at the Institute of Human Development at the University of California, Berkeley, developed the Q-Sort. One of Somers' questionnaires was given to U. C. Berkeley students in 1968, and his other questionnaire went to the parents of these students in 1968. Block's Q-Sort was also given to the parents of these students in 1968.

Somers' student questionnaire was part of a survey of the University of California, Berkeley campus in 1968 associated with his course in research methodology, Sociology 105. This survey is a random sample of all Berkeley students (undergraduates and graduates) registered at Sproul Hall in 1968. It asks many questions that relate to the theories of activism under consideration. The total number of respondents is 492. Respondents include students who had participated in various instances of student activism, which are discussed in Chapter 1 and in Appendix B, as well as students who did not participate in these instances of activism. The students who did participate are called "activists," and those who had the opportunity to participate but did not participate are called "non-activists." There are other students who were not on campus for any of the three instances of activism included in our index of student activism. These students are not included in the calculation of the tables that concern student activism. Only activists and non-activists are included in the calculation of these tables, although in most tables only the figures for activists are reported. The numbers of students who were activists, non-activists, or not on campus for each of the three instances of activism are reported in Appendix B.

Accompanying Somers' 1968 data on students are the two instruments sent to the parents of the U. C. Berkeley undergraduates in the sample —Somers' parental questionnaire and Block's Q-Sort. Both the Somers and Block instruments went to the same parents (they were even sent in the same envelope). The parents of the graduate students in the sample were not sent either instrument.

In general, Somers' parental data are related to the political, economic, and racial attitudes of the parents, as well as their feelings about the education their child was receiving at Berkeley. This is an important questionnaire for many reasons. One of its biggest advantages is that it permits the parents to discuss their own political views, as well as state their own social-economic background. Thus, a "contamination effect" can be avoided because it is not necessary to rely on the students' report of the political views of their parents and possibly confound parental views with their own. For example, it is not impossible that a student could label his parents' views as "conservative" when they consider themselves "liberal." Most of the existing studies of student activism had to rely on the students' report of the politics of their parents whereas we do not. However on occasion we have stated in footnotes where we took the student report on parental background or parental political party affiliation in order to increase the number of cases on which to base percentages. In these instances, we attempted to justify why taking the student report was legitimate. However, with regard to the political and cultural ideology of the parents, we relied exclusively on the parental report of their own views.

The other parental instrument developed by Block is related to childrearing practices and other aspects of parent-child relations when the student was growing up. This instrument should permit a more sophisticated test of the family conflict theory of student activism that is usually possible; certainly these data will permit a better test of Feuer's ideas than he demanded of himself in *The Conflict of Generations*.[1] However, it is not possible to fully test the more subtle aspects of Feuer's argument about unresolved Oedipal crises of student activists (e.g., we do not have data on the present level of repression of hate by the student for the parent of the same sex). We can only approximate a test of Feuer's Freudian approach to activism by getting measures on more gross categories such as parent-child conflict during childhood reported by the parents. But these parental instruments add depth to our study, and they are somewhat unique to the study of activism; only Flacks and a few other investigators have data on both students and their parents.

The student data were collected by student interviewers who were enrolled in Professor Somers' Sociology 105 class in 1968. The parental data were derived from the two instruments, which were mailed to the parents of the students for self-administration. The response rates were quite good for all three instruments. The response rate for Somers' student data was 89 percent. The response rate for Somers' parental data was 65 percent for mothers, 63 percent for the fathers; with an overall response rate of 64 percent. Finally, the response rate for Block's Q-Sort data was 60.2 percent for the mothers, 57.5 percent for the fathers, with an overall response rate of 59 percent. Most questionnaires with interviews do not get as high a response rate as the student questionnaire, and most mailed instruments do not get as high a response rate as these two mailed instruments.

It is possible to argue that the data for the student questionnaire are not as good as it appears because the interviewers were students. It could be said that they were not sufficiently trained or even that some may have cheated on interviews. Although it is impossible to ascertain the exact accuracy of the data, there are arguments and evidence against these charges. First, many of the questions were precoded, which calls for less technical training than uncoded questions. Also, these were largely upper-division college students who had some prior experience with sociological questions and issues. Finally, many of the interviewers had been directly or indirectly involved in campus politics (merely being a student at Berkeley involves a person indirectly). As a result many student interviewers were possibly more sensitized to issues in the questionnaire than more trained, but less involved, professional interviewers.

Professor Somers has spoken at length on the problem of the validity of the data. Somers has stated that: "In the spring of 1965, the staff of the Byrne subcommittee of the Regents of the University of California requested permission to use survey material gathered by my class in 1964 and by Professor Gales's class in 1965. They also asked permission to have the interviews checked for bias by a commercial polling agency. Results of this independent check showed that student interviewers—judging from answers they gave to the same questions—did not bias the results."[2]

The Field Corporation study, strictly speaking, deals only with the 1964 and 1965 data at Berkeley. But if they found that student interviewers did not bias the results during the height of the FSM, then similar student interviewers a few years later would also not be expected to bias the results. This is especially the case since the Berkeley campus was not in the same sort of turmoil during the period when the 1968 interviews were conducted as it was during the FSM, which presumably increases the accuracy of the data.

There is still another point to consider. In this particular sample it would be more difficult than usual for students to "fake" interviews by not asking the respondents, but by filling out the questionnaires themselves. The difficulty arises because corresponding questionnaires had to be sent to the parents of the actual respondents. If the interviewers filled out the questionnaires themselves it would be more difficult, although not impossible, to find out the addresses of the parents of the real respondents. Thus, this type of inaccuracy is probably minimized for the 1968 data.

In addition it should be clear that these same arguments about interviewer bias would not apply to the parental instruments. The parental instruments were entirely self-administered. Hence the absence of student interviewers means the absence of any interviewer bias for the parental data.

Finally, there is a very high correspondence between the sample and the U. C. Berkeley population of 27,749 (the population does not include Boalt

Hall Law students, or any other group of students whose names were not listed in the 30-odd boxes of file cards at Sproul Hall). For example, freshmen and sophomore men accounted for 13.8 percent of the population in 1968 and they were 14.0 percent of the sample. Also, freshmen and sophomore women were 11.2 percent of the population and 13.2 percent of the sample. The only group that was somewhat underrepresented was the male graduate students, who constituted 27.4 percent of the population but only 19.9 percent of the sample. But otherwise, there was an excellent correspondence between sample and population for the 1968 student data.

From these arguments and information about the 1968 student data, we conclude that these data are reliable to an acceptable degree. It seems quite likely that the conclusions drawn from this sample will be a reasonably accurate reflection of the Berkeley student population in 1968. The high response rates of the parental instruments, and the discussion in Chapter 4 that indicates the relative lack of bias between parents who responded versus those who did not respond to the Somers parental questionnaire, suggest that the parental data are quite good also.

There is one final problem that should be addressed with regard to the instruments of Somers and Block we use to test the various theories of student activism. In order to make inferences about the adequacy of the theories under consideration, there must be a fairly close tie-in between the theoretical ideas and the items in the three instruments. If there were little or no relation between the theories examined in this book and the items of the instruments used to operationally define the basic concepts of the theories, then we would have no basis to say we have provided evidence on the adequacy of the theories. However, we think there is sufficient tie-in between the instruments and many basic concepts in the theories. In addition, we have tried to mention the parts of the theories that we felt the instruments could not adequately test. For example, we noted that the more subtle aspects of Feuer's thesis of unresolved Oedipal crises could not be adequately tested by these data. However, the data can be used to make inferences about the adequacy of other parts of the theories. And we have also gathered various types of other data to help test the theories more completely.

It is clear that we have discussed quite different theoretical and ideological perspectives. In fact, all of the perspectives discussed here represent at least somewhat different traditions of explaining activism. We tried to include different perspectives to examine the relative strengths and weaknesses of these different traditions. What is important about all of the traditions is that they attempt to explain a common subject—student activism—in terms of different conceptual frameworks.

The problem for the analyst of the theories is to select items from the instruments that represent the basic concepts from the different traditions

as they have been defined in that tradition. We feel that we have selected
items that are adequate representations of the basic concepts of the traditions considered; the reader can examine the items we have used to form
indices of concepts in Appendix C. For example, when Feuer argues that
family conflicts are associated with activism, we can turn to Block's
instrument for items that very specifically indicate the level of conflict in
the childhood of activists. And when Flacks argues that radical political
consciousness is associated with activism, we can turn to Somers' student
and parental questionnaires for items that very specifically relate to an
individual's ideological position on matters of politics, economics, and race
relations. In fact, when Somers was constructing his student and parental
questionnaires, he had Flacks' ideas about activism in mind to test. Flacks
had sent Somers a pre-publication copy of "The Liberated Generation,"
which Somers took into account when writing the items for his
questionnaires.[3] On the other hand, Block's Q-Sort is a very general
instrument about childrearing patterns. It has been given to various different groups in the last number of years. However, one of the groups it has
been given to is another sample of U. C. Berkeley student activists.[4] Of
course, it is up to the reader to determine how closely the questionnaire and
Q-Sort items of Somers and Block represent the basic concepts of the
theories we are examining. But we think in general that the items selected
do relate well to the basic concepts.

Notes

1. Lewis S. Feuer, *The Conflict of Generations* (New York: Basic
Books, 1969).

2. Robert H. Somers, "The Berkeley Campus in the Twilight of the
Free Speech Movement: Hope or Futility?" in James McEvoy and Abraham Miller, eds., *Black Power and Student Rebellion* (Belmont, California:
Wadsworth Publishing Co., 1969), footnote 5, p. 439. The independent
check on Somers' data was written up as "A critique of two surveys of
student attitudes toward the 'Free Speech' demonstrations on the Berkeley
campus of the University of California," Field Research Corporation, 14
April 1965, unpublished.

3. Somers mentioned the tie-in between his questionnaires and Flacks'
"The Liberated Generation" to me in a private communication. Dr.
Somers is a Research Sociologist at the Institute for Research in Social
Behavior, The Claremont Hotel, Berkeley, California 94705.

4. See Jeanne H. Block, Norma Haan, and M. Brewster Smith,
"Socialization Correlates of Student Activism," *The Journal of Social
Issues* XXV, No. 4 (1969):143-77. The data for this study includes a random

sample of the U. C. Berkeley campus in 1965-66. Students who were arrested in the 1964 Free Speech Movement sit-in at U. C. Berkeley were among those considered student activists, although there were others also considered activists. Actually this study distinguishes between Activists and Dissenters whereas both groups are considered activists in our study (the Dissenters in the Block, Haan, and Smith study engaged in political protests similar to the Activists, but the Dissenters were not as involved in activities of social service as were the Activists). There is a good degree of overlap between their conclusions about activism and our conclusions, although some differences exist. We agree on the finding that student activists tended to have conflictual relations with their parents. It is noteworthy that their Q-Sort study was of the students and our Q-Sort study was of the parents, but the results about conflictual relations are similar. Furthermore, Block has done some analysis of the parental data that we are using and came to the same conclusions as we did about conflictual relations (see their pp. 147, note 2; 169; and 176). There are evidences in the Block, Haan, and Smith study that activists are characterized by some of the non-conventional cultural values we previously discussed, but which we felt were not major conditions of activism. In addition, they demonstrate that activists share a trait with the "Conventionalists" of being raised to become independent, responsible, and mature at an early age. We did not address these latter aspects of childrearing practices directly. Also, they tend to disagree that social conditions, especially a Jewish background, influence socialization practices. We found that Jewish activists tended to be raised in generally democratic and permissive families. Finally, we partly agree and partly disagree on the ideological similarities between activists and their parents. They feel that their category of Activist shares a "Liberal-Radical" perspective with the parents. However, they also feel that their category of Dissenter diverges from the ideology of the parents. Our own study did not distinguish between Activist and Dissenter. However, we found reasonably strong links between parents' radical political consciousness, student's radical political consciousness, and activism. But we found much weaker links between parents' liberal ideology, student's liberal ideology, and activism.

Appendix B
The Index of Student
Political Activism

Here we list the number of students who stated in the 1968 questionnaire that they were active or not active in the three instances of student activism in our index of activism. Also, we list the number of students who did not answer the question concerning their participation, or lack of participation, in the instances of activism. And we additionally list the students who were not on campus during each of the instances of activism:

Free Speech Movement of 1964-65:

Active, 48

Not Active, 83

No Answer, 10

Not on Campus, 351.

Student Strike in December 1966:

Active, 70

Not Active, 195

No Answer, 25

Not on Campus, 202.

Oakland Induction Center Demonstration, Fall 1967:

Active, 75

Not Active, 343

No Answer, 29

Not on Campus, 45.

Appendix C
Items for the Indices of the
Basic Concepts

This Appendix reports the items from the three instruments discussed in Appendix A—the two questionnaires and the Q-Sort—that are used to indicate the basic concepts we have used. Various multiple-item indices, as well as single-item indicators, are reported. The wording of items found in this Appendix is often a paraphrase of the exact wording in the instruments.

The rationale for selecting the specific items is both theoretical and empirical. The items should all fit within the general definitions of the concepts. Most of the concepts are generally defined in the various empirical chapters. The theoretical rationale behind many of these general definitions can be found in our more general discussions of the conditions underlying student activism.

There is no clear statement in the literature on index formation about when to include or exclude items from indices on empirical grounds.[1] Most discussions simply say that some degree of positive association between the items in the index must exist in order to include them in the same index (or negative association, depending on how the items are worded). Also, there is often some statement to the effect that the degree of association between items should not be too high or too low. However, the terms "too high" and "too low" are usually not specified.

It has been suggested that as a "rule of thumb" we include theoretically relevant items in the same index that had Gamma associations between .2 and .8; these are the limits which would avoid being "too high" or "too low."[2] This is the range that we took as a rule of thumb when selecting items for our indices. However, as the figures presented below indicate, we did not always follow the rule "to the letter." The special problem of index formation in this study is that we tried to get items which had Gammas of .2 to .8 for all three types of people involved instead of the more customary single type of person—that is, wherever possible (which was often), we used the identical items to indicate the same concept for the student, his or her mother, and his or her father. Occasionally items would fall within the range of .2 to .8 for students, for example, but would not do so for one or both parents (or vice versa). When this happened, we usually eliminated the items from inclusion in the indices. The only instances where we kept items in the indices that were below .2 or above .8 were situations where the theoretical relevance of the specific items was sufficiently great to justify their inclusion. Fortunately, there were very few instances where the empirical association was somewhat weak or too great. Gamma was a particularly good measure of association to help form our indices because

165

this measure is symetrical. Since these are additive indices, all of the items included in the indices are considered "equal." Of course, no Gamma scores are reported for single-item indicators.

Finally, a word on "cut-off points." Some cutting points are self-explanatory in the presentation of the items below (e.g., the difference between high, moderate, and low grade point average is stated below). However, there are other items whose cut-off points are not obvious as presented. In particular, Somers' items that ask the respondent to agree or disagree, and Block's Q-Sort items require further explanation.

Many items in Somers' questionnaires have four possibilities of agreement or disagreement: strongly agree, agree, disagree, and strongly disagree. We put together (i.e., recoded) those who strongly agreed or agreed with an item, and we also put together those who strongly disagreed or disagreed with an item. We worded this recoding in terms of the familiar dichotomy "Agree-Disagree" as is apparent in the way we present the items below. Occasionally the questionnaires did not give a choice of strongly agree and agree (or strongly disagree and disagree), and we simply used the category agree (or disagree) in these instances. So our cut-off point in general was at the level of "agreement" (or "disagreement") instead of "strong agreement" (or "strong disagreement").

Block's Q-Sort is a seven-point scale going from "most descriptive" to "most undescriptive," with the mid-point of 4 being "neither descriptive nor undescriptive." The 7 categories used for each of the 91 items in the Q-Sort are:

7— Most Descriptive

6— Quite Descriptive

5— Fairly Descriptive

4— Neither Descriptive nor Undescriptive

3— Fairly Undescriptive

2— Quite Undescriptive

1— Most Undescriptive

We combined the first three responses as well as the last three responses, and we omitted responses at the mid-point of 4. Depending on the wording of an item, we called the combination of the first three responses—7, 6, and 5—"High" (or "Low") on a variable such as permissive childrearing. We called the combination of the last three responses—3, 2, and 1—"Low" (or "High") on the same variable. As a result, we derived a dichotomy of descriptive versus undescriptive for the various items in the Q-Sort, and we labeled the dichotomy "High" versus "Low" on the numerous variables.

Below are the Gamma scores for students, mothers, and fathers for the various items in the indices.

Parents' Radical Political Consciousness

1. Five-item index: (1) Agree sweeping economic changes are necessary to solve social problems; (2) Disagree conditions are worsened for Negroes by following advocates of Black Power; (3) Agree that the United States is not sincere in its wishes to negotiate with North Vietnam; (4) Disagree there is a chance for people like me to have any voice in the affairs of the government in Washington; (5) Agree that American society is basically unjust and that revolutionary changes are needed.

2. Gammas for Mothers:

	Economic Changes	Black Power	Vietnam	Government	Revolution
Economic Changes	—	−.526	.653	−.639	.813
Black Power	−.526	—	−.427	.114	−.429
Vietnam	.653	−.427	—	−.525	.640
Government	−.639	.114	−.525	—	−.746
Revolution	.813	−.429	.640	−.746	—

3. Gammas for Fathers:

	Economic Changes	Black Power	Vietnam	Government	Revolution
Economic Changes	—	−.490	.227	−.311	.657
Black Power	−.490	—	−.561	−.039	−.561
Vietnam	.227	−.561	—	−.354	.116
Government	−.331	−.039	−.354	—	−.317
Revolution	.657	−.561	.116	−.317	—

Student Political Activism

1. See Appendix B for items indicating Student Political Activism.
2. No Gamma scores are reported between the three events of activism included in the index because various students were not on campus for all three instances of activism. Thus Gamma scores would be meaningless since only a relatively small number of students had the opportunity to participate in all three instances of activism.

Student's Radical Political Consciousness

1. Five-item index: (1) Agree sweeping economic changes are necessary to solve social problems; (2) Disagree conditions are worsened for Ne-

groes by following advocates of Black Power; (3) Agree that the United States is not sincere in its wishes to negotiate with North Vietnam; (4) Disagree there is a chance for people like me to have any voice in the affairs of the government in Washington; (5) Agree that American society is basically unjust, and that revolutionary changes are needed.

2. Gammas for Students:

	Economic Changes	Black Power	Vietnam	Government	Revolution
Economic Changes	—	−.635	.634	−.326	.801
Black Power	−.635	—	−.640	.182	−.688
Vietnam	.634	−.640	—	−.316	.733
Government	−.326	.182	−.316	—	−.368
Revolution	.801	−.688	.733	−.368	—

Parents' Liberal Political Ideology

1. Four-item index: (1) Agree Negro pressure groups should have more influence in American society; (2) Support extending Medicare to cover everyone; (3) Support giving everyone a guaranteed income; (4) Agree labor unions should have the same or more influence in American society.

2. Gammas for Mothers:

	Negro Groups	Medicare	Guaranteed Income	Labor Unions
Negro Groups	—	.791	.899	.578
Medicare	.791	—	.980	.552
Guaranteed Income	.899	.980	—	.720
Labor Unions	.578	.552	.720	—

3. Gammas for Fathers:

	Negro Groups	Medicare	Guaranteed Income	Labor Unions
Negro Groups	—	.532	.707	.662
Medicare	.532	—	.907	.491
Guaranteed Income	.707	.907	—	.386
Labor Unions	.662	.491	.386	—

Student's Liberal Political Ideology

1. Four-item index: (1) Agree Negro pressure groups should have more influence in American society; (2) Support extending Medicare to cover everyone; (3) Support giving everyone a guaranteed income; (4) Agree Labor Unions should have the same or more influence in American society.

2. Gammas for Students:

	Negro Groups	*Medicare*	*Guaranteed Income*	*Labor Unions*
Negro Groups	—	.460	.581	.413
Medicare	.460	—	.709	.481
Guaranteed Income	.581	.709	—	.303
Labor Unions	.413	.481	.303	—

Student's Educational Reform Political Consciousness (also called *Student's Educational Reform Ideology*)

1. Four-item index: (1) Classes at Berkeley are too large; (2) Students should have more control over educational policies at Berkeley; (3) Most professors at Berkeley are more interested in their research than in their students; (4) The University of California at Berkeley sometimes seems to operate like a factory.

2. Gammas for Students:

	Large Classes	*Student Control*	*Professors' Research*	*U. C. a Factory*
Large Classes	—	.397	.531	.775
Student Control	.397	—	.162	.415
Professors' Research	.531	.162	—	.462
U. C. a Factory	.775	.415	.462	—

Student's Civil Rights Reform Political Consciousness (also called *Student's Civil Rights Reform Ideology*)

1. Two-item index: (1) Non-violent civil disobedience by civil rights groups produces some immediate gains in housing, employment, and transportation for Negroes; (2) Non-violent civil disobedience by civil rights groups can produce full equality for Negroes.

2. Gamma = .695

Parents' Humanitarianism

1. Single-item indicator: (1) It is vital for a growing child to be aware of and concerned about injustice in society.

Student's Humanitarianism

1. Single-item indicator: (1) It is vital for a growing child to be aware of and concerned about injustice in society.

Parents' Democratic Childrearing Practices

1. Three-item index: (1) Child's preferences taken into account by parents in making family plans; (2) Parents permitted child to make many decisions for himself; (3) Disagree that a child should be "seen and not heard."
2. Gammas for Mothers:

	Child's Preferences	Child's Decisions	"Seen, Not Heard"
Child's Preferences	—	.752	−.464
Child's Decisions	.752	—	−.801
"Seen, Not Heard"	−.464	−.801	—

3. Gammas for Fathers:

	Child's Preferences	Child's Decisions	"Seen, Not Heard"
Child's Preferences	—	.724	−.371
Child's Decisions	.724	—	−.776
"Seen, Not Heard"	−.371	−.776	—

Parents' Permissive Childrearing Practices (as measured by Extent of Punishment)

1. Two-item index: (1) Disagree that I taught my child that in one way or another punishment will find him when he is bad; (2) I believe in praising a child when he is good rather than punishing him when he is bad.
2. Gamma for Mothers = −.734
3. Gamma for Fathers = −.280

Parents' Hostility to Child During Childhood

1. Two-item index: (1) I often felt angry with my child; (2) I sometimes teased and made fun of my child.
2. Gamma for Mothers = .469
3. Gamma for Fathers = .604

Parents' Report of Conflict During Childrearing

1. Single-item indicator: (1) There was a good deal of conflict between my child and me.

Parents' Educational Reform Ideology

1. Two-item index: (1) My son or daughter is getting only a "fair" or a poor education at Berkeley; (2) The U. C. Berkeley campus administration cannot be counted on to give sufficient consideration to the rights and needs of students in setting University policy.
2. Gamma for Mothers = .650
3. Gamma for Fathers = .406

Student's Radical-Reform Political Consciousness

1. No Gamma score is involved in this index. The reader should refer to Table 12-1. Those students who are high on both radical political consciousness and educational reform political consciousness are those students who are considered to be high on radical-reform political consciousness.

Parents' Romanticism

1. Two-item index: (1) Warmth and intimacy are among the most important realities of life and children should come to know their importance; (2) The most important goal in life is the full realization of one's unique potential.
2. Gamma for Mothers = .385
3. Gamma for Fathers = .197

Student's Romanticism

1. Two-item index: (1) Warmth and intimacy are among the most important realities of life and children should come to know their importance; (2) The most important goal in life is the full realization of one's unique potential.
2. Gamma = .874

Parents' Intellectualism

1. Three-item index: (1) I respect my child's opinions and encourage him to express them; (2) I encourage my child to wonder and think about life; (3) I feel the freedom to be creative and original is an important value for my child to consider in choosing a future job or profession.

2. Gammas for Mothers:

	Opinions	Thinking	Creativity
Opinions	—	.629	.483
Thinking	.629	—	.496
Creativity	.483	.496	—

3. Gammas for Fathers:

	Opinions	Thinking	Creativity
Opinions	—	.584	.277
Thinking	.584	—	.230
Creativity	.277	.230	—

Student's Intellectualism

1. Two-item index: (1) It is important to me to be able to attend serious concerts, plays, lectures, art shows, and so on at college; (2) I feel that the freedom to be creative and original is an important value for me to consider in choosing a future job or profession.

2. Gamma = .383

Parents' Expressivity of Impulses

1. Three-item index: (1) A young person should feel free to experiment with ways of living and not be too constrained by conventional morality; (2) Disagree that self-restraint is especially necessary for young people; (3) Young people who are too self-controlled may never learn their real nature.

2. Gammas for Mothers:

	Morality	Self-Restraint	Self-Control
Morality	—	−.694	.707
Self-Restraint	−.694	—	−.809
Self-Control	.707	−.809	—

3. Gammas for Fathers:

	Morality	Self-Restraint	Self-Control
Morality	—	−.623	.470
Self-Restraint	−.623	—	−.454
Self-Control	.470	−.454	—

Student's Expressivity of Impulses

1. Three-item index: (1) A young person should feel free to experiment with ways of living and not be too constrained by conventional morality; (2) Disagree that self-restraint is especially necessary for young people; (3) Young people who are too self-controlled may never learn their real nature.

2. Gammas for Students:

	Morality	Self-Restraint	Self-Control
Morality	—	−.762	.405
Self-Restraint	−.762	—	−.465
Self-Control	.405	−.465	—

Parents' Cooperative Values

1. Single-item indicator: (1) Disagree that it is having to compete with others that "keeps a person on his toes."

Student's Cooperative Values

1. Single-item indicator: (1) Disagree that it is having to compete with others that "keeps a person on his toes."

Close or Distant Present Relations Between Parents and Children Reported by Parents

1. Single-item indicator asking parents whether they have close or distant relations with their child now.

Close or Distant Present Relations Between Parents and Children Reported by the Student

1. Single-item indicator asking the student whether he or she has close or distant relations with his or her parents now.

Close or Distant Relations During Childhood Between Parents and Children Reported by Parents

1. Three-item index: (1) I found some of my greatest satisfactions in my child; (2) I was easy going and relaxed with my child; (3) My child and I had warm, intimate times together.
2. Gammas for Mother:

	Satisfactions	Relaxed	Intimate Times
Satisfactions	—	.179	.367
Relaxed	.179	—	.429
Intimate Times	.367	.429	—

3. Gammas for Father:

	Satisfactions	Relaxed	Intimate Times
Satisfactions	—	.165	.649
Relaxed	.165	—	.571
Intimate Times	.649	.571	—

Parental Affection to Child During Childhood Reported by Parents

1. Single-item indicator: (1) It was undescriptive of our family's beliefs that too much affection and tenderness can harm or weaken a child.

Levels of Academic Achievement as Measured by Grade Point Average

1. Single-item indicator asking students their grade point average on a 4.00 scale.
2. High G. P. A. = 3.30-4.00;
   Moderate G. P. A. = 2.50-3.29;
   Low G. P. A. = Under 2.00-2.49.

"Objective" Social Alienation of Students

1. Single-item indicator of student's place of residence categorized in terms of its degree of social isolation (e.g., in an apartment alone versus living with relatives).

"Subjective" Social Alienation of Students

1. Two-item index: (1) Most of the students at Cal seem to be unfriendly; (2) I often feel lonely walking on campus.
2. Gamma = .735

Current Relations with Student (improved, worsened, or no change) Reported by Parents

1. Single-item indicator: (1) In the last year or so, do you feel that your son or daughter has been growing closer or further away from you?

Student's Support for Black Power Ideology

1. Two single-item indicators, which are not formed into an index: (1) Disagree that Negroes will only make things worse for themselves by following advocates of Black Power; (2) Disagree that the strength of the Civil Rights Movement has been weakened by advocates of Black Power.

Student's Opinion that Blacks Will Attain Equality Through Violence

1. Single-item indicator: (1) Negroes have a fair or good chance of gaining full equality by violent rioting.

Student's Opinion that the University of California at Berkeley Is Too Closely Tied to the Existing Political-Economic "Establishment"

1. Single-item indicator: (1) I feel the University is too closely tied to established authorities and interests in American society.

Student's Opinion That He (or She) Would Not Be in School if it Were Not for the Military Draft or Unemployment

1. Single-item indicator: (1) If you didn't have to have a college degree to get a job (add for men only: or wouldn't get drafted if you dropped out), do you think you would still be in college this year?

Male Student's Military Draft Status

1. Single-item indicator: (1) Draft statuses distinguished between I-A (immediately available for duty), II-S (temporary student deferment), and Ineligible for Military Service (only those American citizens who could otherwise be drafted are included in this category—for example, Status II-A who are deferred because of essential civilian employment).

Student's Favorable Attitude Toward Drugs

1. Two-item index: (1) Disagree that marijuana leads to psychological dependence; (2) Agree that marijuana leads to a better outlook on the world.
2. Gamma $= -.515$.

Student's Favorable Attitude Toward "Hippies"

1. Three-item index: (1) If "hippies" had an effect on American life and culture, it would be beneficial; (2) "Hippies" will have their life enriched for their experiences; (3) Disagree that "hippies" are mostly lazy people shirking responsibility.
2. Gammas for Students:

	Cultural Benefit	Life Enriched	Not Lazy
Cultural Benefit	—	.741	−.501
Life Enriched	.741	—	−.460
Not Lazy	−.501	−.460	—

Single-item indicators of various *Social-Economic Background* variables such as family income are presented in Table 9-1.

Notes

1. For example, see Jum C. Nunnaly, *Psychometric Theory* (New York: McGraw-Hill Book Co., 1967), Chapter 3, pp. 75-102.

2. Private communication from Dr. Robert H. Somers. Dr. Somers is a Research Sociologist at the Institute for Research in Social Behavior, The Claremont Hotel, Berkeley, California 94705. For a discussion of Gamma, see William L. Hays, *Statistics for Psychologists* (New York: Holt, Rinehart and Winston, 1963), pp. 655-6.

Bibliography

Apter, David E., ed. *Ideology and Discontent*. New York: The Free Press, 1964.

————. "Introduction: Ideology and Discontent," in David E. Apter, ed., *Ideology and Discontent*. New York: The Free Press, 1964, pp. 15-46.

Baran, Paul A. and Paul M. Sweezy. *Monopoly Capital*. New York: Monthly Review Press, 1966.

Blauner, Robert. "Whitewash Over Watts," *Trans-action* 3 (March-April 1966): 3-9, 54.

Block, Jeanne H., Norma Haan, and M. Brewster Smith. "Socialization Correlates of Student Activism," *The Journal of Social Issues* XXV, No. 4 (1969): 143-77.

Braungart, Richard G. "Family Status, Socialization, and Student Politics: A Multivariate Analysis," *American Journal of Sociology* 77 (July 1971): 108-30.

Brinton, Crane. *The Anatomy of Revolution*. New York: W. W. Norton & Co., 1938.

Bulletin of the University of California, Berkeley, *Campus Anti-Imperialist Coalition*, Vol. I, No. 6, May 1, 1972.

Carmichael, Stokely and Charles V. Hamilton. *Black Power: The Politics of Liberation in America*. New York: Vintage Books, A Division of Random House, 1967.

Cockburn, Alexander and Robin Blackburn, eds. *Student Power: Problems, Diagnosis, Action*. Baltimore: Penguin Books, in association with *New Left Review*, 1969.

Cook, Theirrie and Michael P. Lerner. "The New American Movement," *Social Policy* 3 (July-August 1972): 27-31, 54-56.

Crews, Frederick. "The Radical Students," book review of Lewis S. Feuer, *The Conflict of Generations*, *The New York Review of Books*, Vol. XII, No. 8, April 24, 1969, pp. 29-34.

Draper, Hal. *Berkeley: The New Student Revolt*. New York: Grove Press, 1965.

Dunlap, Riley. "A Comment on 'Multiversity, University Size, University Quality, and Student Protest: An Empirical Study'," *American Sociological Review* 35 (June 1970): 525-28.

————. "Radical and Conservative Student Activists: A Comparison of Family Backgrounds," *Pacific Sociological Review* 13 (Summer 1970): 171-81.

177

Durkheim, Emile. *The Division of Labor in Society,* translated by George Simpson. London: Collier-Macmillan Limited, The Free Press of Glencoe, 1964. Originally published in 1893.

Feldman, Kenneth A. and Theodore M. Newcomb. *The Impact of College on Students.* San Francisco: Jossey-Bass, 1969. Volume I: *An Analysis of Four Decades of Research;* Volume II: *Summary Tables.*

Feuer, Lewis S. *The Conflict of Generations.* New York: Basic Books, 1969.

Field Research Corporation. "A Critique of Two Surveys of Student Attitudes Toward the 'Free Speech' Demonstrations on the Berkeley Campus of the University of California," 14 April 1965, unpublished.

Finney, Henry C. "Political Libertarianism at Berkeley: An Application of Perspectives from the New Student Left." *The Journal of Social Issues* 27, No. 1 (1971): 35-61.

Flacks, Richard. "Towards a Socialist Sociology: Some Proposals for Work in the Coming Period," *The Insurgent Sociologist,* Vol. II, No. 2 (January-February 1971): 12-27.

―――――. "The New Left and American Politics After Ten Years," *The Journal of Social Issues* 27, No. 1 (1971): 21-34.

―――――. *Youth and Social Change.* Chicago: Markham Publishing Co., 1971.

―――――. "Review Article: Feuer's *Conflict of Generations,*" *Journal of Social History* 4 (Winter 1970-71): 141-53.

―――――. "Social and Cultural Meanings of Student Revolt: Some Informal Comparative Observations," *Social Problems* 17 (Winter 1970): 340-57.

―――――. "The Liberated Generation: An Exploration of the Roots of Student Protest," *The Journal of Social Issues* 23 (July 1967): 52-75.

―――――. "Strategies for Radical Social Change," *Social Policy* 1 (March-April 1971): 7-14.

―――――. and Milton Mankoff. "Revolt in Santa Barbara: Why They Burned the Bank," *The Nation* 210, March 23, 1970, pp. 337-40.

Freud, Sigmund. *Totem and Taboo,* Authorized translation by James Strachey. New York: W. W. Norton & Co., 1950.

―――――. *Group Psychology and the Analysis of the Ego,* Translated by James Strachey. New York: Bantam Books, 1921, 1960.

Geertz, Clifford. "Ideology as a Cultural System," in David E. Apter, ed., *Ideology and Discontent.* New York: The Free Press, 1964, pp. 47-76.

Gintis, Herbert. "The New Working Class and Revolutionary Youth," *Continuum* 8 (Spring-Summer 1970): 151-174.

Glock, Charles Y., ed. *Survey Research in the Social Sciences.* New York: Russell Sage Foundation, 1967.

Goldsen, Rose K., Morris Rosenberg, Robin M. Williams, Jr., and Edward A. Suchman. *What College Students Think*. Princeton, New Jersey: D. Van Nostrand Co., 1960.

Hays, William L. *Statistics for Psychologists*. New York: Holt, Rinehart and Winston, 1963.

Heirich, Max and Sam Kaplan. "Yesterday's Discord," in Seymour Martin Lipset and Sheldon S. Wolin, eds., *The Berkeley Student Revolt*. Garden City, N. Y.: Anchor Books, 1965, pp. 10-35.

Hirschi, Travis and Hanan C. Selvin. *Delinquency Research: An Appraisal of Analytic Methods*. New York: The Free Press, 1967.

Hirschi, Travis and Joseph Zelan. "Student Activism: A Critical Review of the Literature and Preliminary Analysis of the Carnegie Commission Data on Graduate Students," unpublished paper.

Horowitz, David. "The Marxist Vision—A Re-Appraisal," in the This World section of the *San Francisco Sunday Examiner & Chronicle,* July 13, 1969, pp. 34, 39.

_____. *Student: The Political Activities of the Berkeley Students*. New York: Ballantine Books, 1962.

Hyman, Herbert. *Survey Design and Analysis*. Copyright 1955 by The Free Press.

Jacobs, Paul and Saul Landau. *The New Radicals*. New York: Random House, 1966.

Keniston, Kenneth. "A Second Look At The Uncommitted," *Social Policy* (July-August 1971): 6-19.

_____. *Youth and Dissent*. New York: Harcourt Brace Jovanovich, 1971.

_____. "The Sources of Student Dissent," in Neil J. Smelser and William T. Smelser, eds., *Personality and Social Systems,* Second Edition. New York: John Wiley and Sons, 1970. pp. 678-700.

_____. *Young Radicals*. New York: Harcourt, Brace & World, 1968.

_____ and Michael Lerner. "Selected References on Student Protest," *The Annals of the American Academy of Political and Social Science* 395 (May 1971): 184-94. Special Editors of this volume on "Student Protest" are Philip G. Altbach and Robert S. Laufer.

Kerr, Clark. *The Uses of the University*. Cambridge, Mass. Harvard University Press, 1964.

Kornhauser, William. *The Politics of Mass Society*. The Free Press of Glencoe, 1959.

Lenin, V. I. *What Is To Be Done?* New York: International Publishers, originally published in 1902, published in the United States in 1929.

Lerner, Michael P. *The New Socialist Revolution*. New York: Delacorte Press, 1973.

Lichtheim, George. "The Concept of Ideology," in George Lichtheim, *The Concept of Ideology and Other Essays*. New York: Vintage Books, A Division of Random House, 1967, pp. 3-46.

Lipset, Seymour Martin. *Rebellion in the University*. Boston: Little, Brown & Co., 1972.

————. "The Activists: A Profile," *The Public Interest* No. 13 (Fall 1968): 39-51. Copyright © by National Affairs, Inc., 1968.

————. "University Student Politics," in Seymour Martin Lipset and Sheldon S. Wolin, eds., *The Berkeley Student Revolt*. Garden City, N.Y.: Anchor Books, 1965, pp. 1-9.

————. *Political Man*. New York: Doubleday & Company, Inc., 1959, 1960.

————and Philip G. Altbach. "Student Politics and Higher Education in the United States," *Comparative Education Review* 10 (June 1966): 320-349.

————and Sheldon S. Wolin, eds. *The Berkeley Student Revolt*. Garden City, N.Y.: Anchor Books, 1965.

Lyonns, Glen. "The Police Car Demonstration: A Survey of Participants," in Seymour Martin Lipset and Sheldon S. Wolin, eds., *The Berkeley Student Revolt*. Garden City, N.Y.: Anchor Books, 1965. pp. 519-30.

Mallet, Serge, *La Nouvelle Classe Ouvrière*. (Paris: Éditions du Seuil, 1963).

Mankoff, Milton and Richard Flacks. "The Changing Social Base of the American Student Movement," *The Annals of The American Academy of Political and Social Science* 395 (May 1971): 54-67. Special Editors of this volume on "Student Protest" are Philip G. Altbach and Robert S. Laufer.

Mankoff, Milton L. "The Political Socialization of Radicals and Militants in the Wisconsin Student Movement During the 1960s," unpublished Ph.D. dissertation, Department of Sociology, University of Wisconsin, 1969.

Marcuse, Herbert. "The Movement in a New Era of Repression: An Assessment," *Berkeley Journal of Sociology: A Critical Review* XVI (1971-1972): 1-14.

————. *An Essay on Liberation*. Boston: Beacon Press, 1969.

Mauss, Armand L. "The Lost Promise of Reconciliation: New Left vs. Old Left," *The Journal of Social Issues* 27, No.1 (1971): 1-20.

————. "On Being Strangled by the Stars and Stripes: The New Left, the

Old Left, and the Natural History of American Radical Movements,'' *The Journal of Social Issues* 27, No. 1 (1971): 183-202.

Merton, Robert K. *Social Theory and Social Structure,* Revised and Enlarged Edition. London: The Free Press of Glencoe, Collier-Macmillan Limited, 1957, originally published in 1949.

Meyer, Marshall W. ''Harvard Students in the Midst of Crisis,'' *Sociology of Education* 44 (Summer 1971): 245-69.

Miller, S. M., Martin Rein, Pamela Roby, and Bertram M. Gross. ''Poverty, Inequality, and Conflict,'' *The Annals of The American Academy of Political and Social Science* 373 (September 1967): 16-52.

Mills, C. Wright. *The Power Elite.* New York: Oxford University Press, A Galaxy Book, 1956, 1965.

Nunnaly, Jum C. *Psychometric Theory.* New York: McGraw-Hill Book Co., 1967.

Oglesby, Carl, ed. *The New Left Reader.* New York: Grove Press, 1969.

Parsons, Talcott and Gerald M. Platt, with the collaboration of Neil J. Smelser. *The American University* (Cambridge, Mass.: Harvard University Press, 1973).

_____and Gerald M. Platt. ''Age, Social Structure, and Socialization in Higher Education,'' *Sociology of Education* 43 (Winter 1970): 1-37.

Peterson, Richard E. ''Goals for California Higher Education: A Survey of 116 Academic Communities,'' Sacramento, California: California Legislature, Assembly Post Office Box 83, State Capitol, March, 1973.

Pinard, Maurice. *The Rise of a Third Party: A Study in Crisis Politics.* Englewood Cliffs, N.J.: Prentice-Hall, 1971.

Pinkney, Alphonso. *The Committed: White Activists in the Civil Rights Movement.* New Haven: College and University Press, 1968.

Ridgeway, James. *The Closed Corporation.* New York: Random House, 1968.

Rieff, Philip. *Freud: The Mind of the Moralist.* Garden City, N.Y.: Anchor Books, 1959, 1961.

Rosenberg, Morris. *The Logic of Survey Analysis.* New York: Basic Books, 1968.

Roszak, Theodore. *The Making of a Counter Culture.* Garden City, N.Y.: Anchor Books, 1969.

Rowntree, John and Margaret. ''The Political Economy of Youth: Youth as Class,'' published by *The Radical Education Project,* Box 625, Ann Arbor, Michigan 48107, pp. 1-36; it also appeared in *Our Generation,* Vol. 6, Nos. 1-2.

Savio, Mario. "Introduction" to Hal Draper, *Berkeley: The New Student Revolt*. New York: Grove Press, 1965, pp. 1-7.

————. "An End to History," in Seymour Martin Lipset and Sheldon S. Wolin, eds., *The Berkeley Student Revolt*. Garden City, N.Y.: Anchor Books, 1965, pp. 216-219.

Schwab, Joseph J. *College Curriculum and Student Protest*. Chicago: The University of Chicago Press, 1969.

Scott, Joseph W. "A Comment on 'Student Protest'," *American Sociological Review* 35 (June 1970): 528-30.

————and Mohamed El-Assal. "Multiversity, University Size, University Quality and Student Protest: An Empirical Study," *American Sociological Review* 34 (October 1969): 702-9.

Skolnick, Jerome H. *The Politics of Protest*. New York: Ballantine Books, 1969.

Smelser, Neil J. "Growth, Structural Change, and Conflict in California Public Higher Education, 1950-1970," in Neil J. Smelser and Gabriel Almond, eds., *Public Higher Education in California*. Berkeley: University of California Press, forthcoming.

————. "Social and Psychological Dimensions of Collective Behavior," in his *Essays in Sociological Explanation*. Englewood Cliffs, N.J.: Prentice-Hall, 1968, pp. 92-121.

————. *Theory of Collective Behavior*. New York: The Free Press of Glencoe, 1963.

————and William T. Smelser. Part One, "Introduction: Analyzing Personality and Social Systems," in Neil J. Smelser and William T. Smelser, eds., *Personality and Social Systems*, 2nd Edition. New York: John Wiley and Sons, 1970, pp. 1-22.

Somers, Robert H. "The Berkeley Campus in the Twilight of the Free Speech Movement: Hope or Futility?" in James McEvoy and Abraham Miller, eds., *Black Power and Student Rebellion*. Belmont, California: Wadsworth Publishing Co., 1969. pp. 419-440.

————. "The Mainsprings of the Rebellion: A Survey of Berkeley Students in November, 1964," in Seymour Martin Lipset and Sheldon S. Wolin, eds., *The Berkeley Student Revolt*. Garden City, N.Y.: Anchor Books, 1965, pp. 530-557.

Stark, Rodney. "Protest + Police = Riot," in James McEvoy and Abraham Miller, eds., *Black Power and Student Rebellion*. Belmont, California: Wadsworth Publishing Co., 1969, pp. 167-96.

————. *Police Riots: Collective Violence and Law Enforcement*. Belmont, California: Wadsworth Publishing Co., 1972.

The American Assembly Columbia University. *The Federal Government and Higher Education*. Englewood Cliffs, N.J.: Prentice-Hall, 1960.

The President's Commission on Campus Unrest. *Campus Unrest.* Washington, D.C.: U.S. Government Printing Office, 1970.

Thompson, E.P. *The Making of the English Working Class.* New York: Pantheon Books, A Division of Random House, 1963, 1964.

Trotsky, Leon. *The Russian Revolution.* Selected and edited by F. W. Dupee from Leon Trotsky, *The History of the Russian Revolution.* Garden City, N.Y.: Anchor Books, 1932, 1959.

Wallerstein, Immanuel and Paul Starr, eds. *The University Crisis Reader: The Liberal University Under Attack.* Volume One. New York: Vintage Books, A Division of Random House, 1971.

Westby, David and Richard Braungart. "Activists and the History of the Future," in Julian Foster and Durward Long, eds., *Protest!: Student Activism in America.* New York: William Morrow & Co., 1970, pp. 158-83.

Wood, James L. *Political Consciousness and Student Activism.* Beverly Hills: Sage Publications, in press.

—————. *Political Consciousness as Reflected in the Literature of the New Left.* Beverly Hills: Sage Publications, forthcoming.

Zelan, Joseph. "Undergraduate Student Activism," July 1971, unpublished paper.

Index

About the Author

James L. Wood is lecturer in the Department of Sociology at the University of California, Riverside. He received the B.A., M.A. and Ph.D. degrees from the Department of Sociology at the University of California, Berkeley. His articles have appeared in *Human Organization* and the *Berkeley Journal of Sociology;* he also served as coeditor of the latter. He is coauthor with Gary T. Marx of "Strands of Theory and Research in Collective Behavior" (*Annual Review of Sociology,* forthcoming), and author of *Political Consciousness and Student Activism* and *Political Consciousness as Reflected in the Literature of the New Left* (Sage Publications, in press).